Political Fallout and Resignations: A Deep Dive Into Financial Scandals

Copyright Page

TITLE: Political Fallout and Resignations: A Deep Dive into Financial Scandals

1ST Edition

Copyright @ 2023

ISBN: 9798223880561

Table of Contents

Political Fallouts and Resignations: A Deep Dive Into Financial Scandals

By Roberto Miguel Rodriguez

Chapter 1: Impact on Global Financial Regulations

The Need for Global Financial Regulations

In recent years, numerous financial scandals have rocked the global economy, leading to severe consequences for not only the financial sector but also for international relations, public perception, and social and economic inequality. The need for global financial regulations has become abundantly clear, as these scandals have exposed the vulnerabilities and loopholes within the existing regulatory frameworks, allowing for widespread corruption, money laundering, and offshore tax havens. This subchapter delves into the pressing reasons why bank regulators must prioritize the establishment and enforcement of global financial regulations.

One of the most significant impacts of financial scandals is the erosion of trust and confidence in the global financial system. The consequences for offshore tax havens have been particularly severe, as these jurisdictions have been exposed as facilitators of illicit financial activities. The revelation of these offshore tax havens has not only led to political fallout and resignations but has also necessitated legal actions and prosecutions to hold the responsible parties accountable.

The scandals have also shed light on the urgent need for reforms in corporate transparency and accountability. It has become evident that the lack of transparency and oversight within corporations has allowed for unethical practices and financial misconduct to go unnoticed for years. Global financial regulations should aim to enhance transparency, ensuring that corporations are held accountable for their actions and that financial reporting is accurate and reliable.

Furthermore, the exposure of these scandals has brought to the forefront the issue of social and economic inequality. The public has become increasingly aware of the vast disparities between the wealthy elite and the rest of society. The need for global financial regulations is crucial in addressing these inequalities, as they can help reduce the concentration of wealth and promote fairer distribution of resources.

The role of whistleblowers and investigative journalism cannot be underestimated in uncovering these financial scandals. Global financial regulations should provide protection and incentives for whistleblowers, encouraging them to come forward with information and ensuring their safety. Investigative journalism also plays a vital role in exposing corruption and wrongdoing, and regulations should support and protect the freedom of the press.

The effects of financial scandals extend beyond national borders and have significant implications for international relations and diplomacy. These scandals can strain diplomatic relations, undermine trust between nations, and hinder cooperation on financial matters. Global financial regulations can help create a level playing field, ensuring that all countries adhere to the same standards and reducing the potential for conflicts arising from financial misconduct.

Finally, the scandals have had a profound impact on the public perception of wealth and privilege. The revelations of widespread corruption and tax evasion have created a sense of outrage among the general public, leading to increased scrutiny of the wealthy and a demand for greater accountability. Global financial regulations can help address these concerns by promoting transparency, fairness, and ethical behavior within the financial sector.

In conclusion, the need for global financial regulations is undeniable. The impact of financial scandals on global financial regulations, offshore tax havens, political fallout, legal actions, corporate transparency, social and economic inequality, whistleblowers, international relations, public perception, money laundering, and corruption cannot be ignored. It is imperative that bank regulators prioritize the establishment and enforcement of global financial regulations to restore trust, promote fairness, and safeguard the global financial system.

Historical Context of Financial Scandals

Understanding the historical context of financial scandals is crucial for bank regulators in order to effectively address and prevent such occurrences in the future. This subchapter delves into the historical backdrop of financial scandals, shedding light on their impact on global financial regulations, consequences for offshore tax havens, political fallout and resignations, legal actions and prosecutions, reforms in corporate transparency and accountability, social and economic inequality exposed, the role of whistleblowers and investigative journalism, effects on international relations and diplomacy, public perception of wealth and privilege, as well as implications for money laundering and corruption.

Financial scandals are not a recent phenomenon but have a long history dating back centuries. From the South Sea Bubble in the 18th century to the Enron scandal in the early 2000s, these scandals have shaped the way financial regulations are implemented globally. They have highlighted the need for stricter oversight and regulations to protect investors and prevent fraudulent activities.

One significant consequence of financial scandals is the exposure of offshore tax havens. These scandals have brought to light the role these tax havens play in facilitating illicit financial activities, leading to calls for greater transparency and regulation in these jurisdictions. Regulators must consider the loopholes that exist in offshore tax havens to prevent money laundering and tax evasion.

The political fallout and resignations resulting from financial scandals have far-reaching implications. These scandals often lead to public outrage, eroding trust in financial institutions and political leaders. The subchapter examines how political systems are affected by these scandals, including the resignation of key figures and the subsequent demands for accountability.

Legal actions and prosecutions are an essential aspect of addressing financial scandals. Regulators need to understand the legal framework surrounding these scandals and the challenges faced in prosecuting those responsible. This subchapter explores the legal implications and the measures taken to hold individuals and corporations accountable.

Reforms in corporate transparency and accountability are often a direct response to financial scandals. Regulators can learn from past scandals to implement measures that promote transparency and ensure companies are held accountable for their actions. The subchapter discusses various reforms and initiatives taken to enhance corporate governance and prevent future scandals.

Financial scandals often expose the stark social and economic inequality present in societies. Regulators must consider the implications of these scandals on societal dynamics and work towards creating a more equitable financial system.

The role of whistleblowers and investigative journalism in uncovering financial scandals cannot be underestimated. This subchapter emphasizes the importance of protecting whistleblowers and fostering investigative journalism to prevent and detect fraudulent activities.

Financial scandals can have severe effects on international relations and diplomacy. This section highlights how scandals can strain relationships between countries and impact their economic cooperation.

Public perception of wealth and privilege is often shaped by financial scandals. Regulators must be aware of the impact these scandals have on public sentiment and work towards restoring trust in the financial system.

Finally, financial scandals have significant implications for money laundering and corruption. Regulators must understand how these scandals contribute to these illicit activities and implement measures to combat them effectively.

In conclusion, this subchapter provides a comprehensive overview of the historical context of financial scandals and their implications for bank regulators. By exploring the impact on global financial regulations, consequences for offshore tax havens, political fallout and resignations, legal actions and prosecutions, reforms in corporate transparency and accountability, social and economic inequality exposed, the role of whistleblowers and investigative journalism, effects on international relations and diplomacy, public perception of wealth and privilege, and implications for money laundering and corruption, regulators can gain valuable insights to prevent future scandals and ensure a more transparent and accountable financial system.

Case Studies: Notable Financial Scandals and Their Impact on Regulations

Financial scandals have long been a source of concern for bank regulators worldwide. These scandals not only erode public trust in the financial system but also expose vulnerabilities in regulations and oversight mechanisms. This subchapter delves into some of the most notable financial scandals in recent history, exploring their far-reaching impact on global financial regulations and various related niches.

One such scandal that sent shockwaves through the financial world was the collapse of Lehman Brothers in 2008. This event not only triggered a global financial crisis but also exposed the need for stricter regulations on risk management and the supervision of financial institutions. As a direct consequence, the Dodd-Frank Act was enacted in the United States, introducing significant reforms to enhance transparency and accountability in the banking sector.

Another case study that highlighted the consequences for offshore tax havens was the Panama Papers scandal in 2016. This leak of confidential documents from a Panamanian law firm exposed the widespread use of tax havens by politicians, celebrities, and wealthy individuals to evade taxes and conceal ill-gotten wealth. The revelations from this scandal prompted regulators to tighten regulations on offshore financial centers, promoting greater transparency and cooperation in tax matters.

Financial scandals often lead to political fallout and resignations, as public outrage demands accountability from those responsible. The scandal involving the Malaysian state investment fund, 1MDB, led to the downfall of former Prime Minister Najib Razak and exposed the extent of corruption and money laundering. This case study underscores the importance of legal actions and prosecutions in holding individuals and institutions accountable for their actions.

In response to these scandals, reforms in corporate transparency and accountability have become imperative. The Enron scandal in the early 2000s shed light on the need for more robust corporate governance practices. This prompted regulators to introduce stricter reporting requirements, independent audits, and enhanced oversight to prevent similar fraudulent activities in the future.

Financial scandals have also exposed the social and economic inequalities that exist within societies. The Occupy Wall Street movement, inspired by the 2008 financial crisis, drew attention to the growing wealth gap and the privileges enjoyed by the financial elite.

These revelations have fueled public debates on income inequality and prompted regulators to consider measures that address this issue more effectively.

Whistleblowers and investigative journalism have played a crucial role in uncovering financial scandals and bringing them to light. The case of Swiss banker Rudolf Elmer, who leaked documents exposing tax evasion by prominent individuals, highlights the significance of these actors in exposing illicit activities and advocating for regulatory changes.

The effects of financial scandals are not limited to the domestic front but also impact international relations and diplomacy. The LIBOR scandal, where several major banks were found to have manipulated the benchmark interest rate, strained trust between financial institutions and governments. This case study emphasizes the need for international cooperation and coordination in regulatory efforts to prevent cross-border financial misconduct.

Public perception of wealth and privilege is invariably influenced by financial scandals. The public's trust in the financial system is eroded when scandals reveal the extent of corruption and malpractice. Regulators must address this by implementing reforms that demonstrate their commitment to protecting the interests of the general public.

Lastly, financial scandals have significant implications for money laundering and corruption. The scandal involving the Malaysian sovereign wealth fund, 1MDB, highlighted the ease with which illicit funds can be laundered through complex financial transactions. Regulators must, therefore, prioritize strengthening anti-money laundering measures and fostering international cooperation in combating financial crimes.

In conclusion, financial scandals have had a profound impact on global financial regulations and various related niches. Through an examination of notable case studies, this subchapter highlights the consequences for offshore tax havens, political fallout and resignations, legal actions and prosecutions, reforms in corporate transparency and accountability, social and economic inequality, the role of whistleblowers and investigative journalism, effects on international relations and diplomacy, public perception of wealth and privilege, and implications for money laundering and corruption. By learning from these scandals, regulators can work towards a more transparent, accountable, and resilient financial system.

Enron Scandal: Shaping Corporate Governance Rules

The Enron scandal, which unfolded in the early 2000s, stands as a watershed moment in the world of corporate governance. This subchapter delves into the significant impact the scandal had on shaping corporate governance rules, specifically addressing the concerns and interests of bank regulators.

The Enron scandal exposed major flaws in the existing regulatory framework, highlighting the dire need for comprehensive reforms. Bank regulators, responsible for overseeing financial institutions and ensuring their compliance with laws and regulations, were particularly affected by the fallout of the scandal.

The Enron scandal had far-reaching consequences for global financial regulations. It demonstrated the inadequacy of existing rules in addressing the complex financial structures and intricate accounting practices employed by Enron. As a result, bank regulators worldwide were compelled to strengthen their oversight mechanisms and update existing regulations to enhance transparency and accountability.

The scandal also shed light on the role of offshore tax havens in facilitating illicit financial activities. Enron utilized complex offshore structures to manipulate its financial statements, evading taxes and hiding its true financial position. Bank regulators recognized the urgent need to crack down on these tax havens and introduced stricter regulations to curb their misuse.

The Enron scandal triggered a wave of political fallout and resignations, as public trust in corporate leadership was severely eroded. This subchapter explores the consequences of these resignations, both in terms of accountability and organizational restructuring within financial institutions. It also examines the legal actions and prosecutions that followed, as regulators sought justice for the stakeholders who suffered from Enron's fraudulent practices.

The Enron scandal prompted a fundamental shift in corporate transparency and accountability. Regulators recognized the importance of enhanced disclosure requirements, stricter auditing standards, and independent oversight to prevent future scandals. This subchapter explores the reforms implemented in corporate governance frameworks to ensure greater transparency and accountability, thereby restoring public trust in the financial system.

Furthermore, the Enron scandal exposed stark social and economic inequalities. The company's executives, while engaging in fraudulent activities, were amassing immense wealth, while employees and investors suffered significant losses. This subchapter delves into the consequences of these revelations, including public outrage and demands for wealth redistribution.

The role of whistleblowers and investigative journalism in exposing the Enron scandal cannot be overstated. Bank regulators must understand the vital role played by these actors in uncovering corporate wrongdoing and ensuring accountability. This subchapter highlights the significance of protecting whistleblowers and encouraging investigative journalism as powerful tools in maintaining a robust corporate governance system.

The Enron scandal had implications for international relations and diplomacy, as the fraudulent activities extended beyond national borders. This subchapter explores the effects of the scandal on international cooperation in combating money laundering and corruption, emphasizing the need for global collaboration in addressing these challenges.

Additionally, the public perception of wealth and privilege was profoundly impacted by the Enron scandal. The lavish lifestyles of Enron executives, juxtaposed with the financial ruin faced by employees and investors, sparked a broader conversation about wealth inequality and the ethics of corporate leadership.

Lastly, the Enron scandal had implications for money laundering and corruption. The subchapter examines the lessons learned from the scandal and the subsequent measures taken to strengthen the fight against illicit financial activities, including tightening regulations, improving enforcement, and enhancing international cooperation.

In conclusion, the Enron scandal shook the foundations of corporate governance and left a lasting impact on bank regulators. This subchapter explores the wide-ranging consequences of the scandal, from global financial regulations to offshore tax havens, political fallout, legal actions, corporate transparency, social and economic inequality, whistleblowers, international relations, public perception, and money laundering. It underscores the imperative for bank regulators to learn from the Enron scandal and continuously adapt and strengthen their regulatory frameworks to prevent future financial scandals.

2008 Financial Crisis: Strengthening Regulatory Frameworks

The 2008 financial crisis was a watershed moment in the history of global finance, exposing significant weaknesses in regulatory frameworks and leading to a series of unprecedented consequences. This subchapter explores the impact of the crisis on various aspects of the financial industry and the subsequent efforts to strengthen regulatory frameworks.

Impact on Global Financial Regulations:

The 2008 financial crisis highlighted the urgent need for stronger global financial regulations. It exposed flaws in risk management practices, inadequate capital requirements, and the lack of oversight in complex financial products. As a result, international bodies such as the Financial Stability Board and the Basel Committee on Banking Supervision were established to enhance coordination and establish stricter regulatory standards.

Consequences for Offshore Tax Havens:

The financial crisis also shed light on the role of offshore tax havens in facilitating tax evasion, money laundering, and illicit financial flows. In response, countries around the world started to tighten regulations on these jurisdictions, increasing transparency and cooperation in the exchange of tax information. The crisis served as a catalyst for a global crackdown on tax havens, reducing their attractiveness for individuals and corporations seeking to evade taxes.

Political Fallout and Resignations:

The crisis triggered a wave of political fallout, with public outrage directed towards the financial sector's recklessness and the perceived lack of accountability. Several high-profile resignations and dismissals occurred as a result, as regulators and policymakers faced intense scrutiny for their perceived failures in preventing the crisis. This led to a demand for greater transparency, ethics, and responsibility in the financial industry.

Legal Actions and Prosecutions:

In the aftermath of the crisis, regulatory bodies and law enforcement agencies initiated legal actions and prosecutions against individuals and institutions involved in fraudulent and unethical practices. This sent a strong message that wrongdoing would not go unpunished, leading to significant fines and settlements. These legal actions aimed to restore public trust and deter future misconduct.

Reforms in Corporate Transparency and Accountability:

The financial crisis prompted a reevaluation of corporate transparency and accountability. Companies were now required to provide more detailed information on their financial positions, risk exposures, and governance structures. Enhanced reporting standards and stricter auditing requirements were implemented to ensure greater transparency and prevent a repeat of the crisis.

Social and Economic Inequality Exposed:

The crisis exposed the deep-rooted social and economic inequalities within societies. The disproportionate impact on vulnerable populations, as well as the massive wealth transfer from taxpayers to bailed-out financial institutions, sparked public outrage. This highlighted the urgent need for policies addressing income inequality, access to credit, and social safety nets.

Role of Whistleblowers and Investigative Journalism:

Whistleblowers and investigative journalists played a crucial role in uncovering the misconduct and systemic flaws that contributed to the crisis. Their courageous actions helped expose corruption, fraud, and unethical practices, leading to greater public awareness and pressure for regulatory reforms.

Effects on International Relations and Diplomacy:

The financial crisis strained international relations and cooperation. Countries engaged in blame games, accusing each other of lax regulations and unfair practices. This prompted a reassessment of global financial governance and the need for stronger international coordination to prevent future crises.

Public Perception of Wealth and Privilege:

The crisis shattered the public's perception of wealth and privilege in the financial sector. The excessive risk-taking and lavish lifestyles of bankers and executives contributed to a widespread perception of greed and entitlement. This led to a fundamental shift in public attitudes towards the financial industry and a demand for a more responsible and ethical approach.

Implications for Money Laundering and Corruption:

The crisis exposed vulnerabilities in anti-money laundering and anti-corruption efforts. It revealed how illicit funds could be channeled through the global financial system, highlighting the need for more robust regulations and enforcement mechanisms. Governments and regulatory bodies responded by strengthening their anti-money laundering frameworks and improving international cooperation.

In conclusion, the 2008 financial crisis had far-reaching implications for regulatory frameworks and the global financial industry. It exposed weaknesses in risk management practices, triggered a wave of political fallout and resignations, and prompted legal actions and prosecutions. The crisis also led to reforms in corporate transparency and accountability, exposed social and economic inequality, and highlighted the crucial role of whistleblowers and investigative journalism. It strained international relations, changed public perception of wealth and privilege, and called for stronger measures against money laundering and corruption. The lessons learned from this crisis have shaped the regulatory landscape, paving the way for a more robust and accountable financial system.

The Role of International Organizations in Establishing Financial Regulations

In the wake of numerous financial scandals that have rocked the global economy, the role of international organizations in establishing financial regulations has come under scrutiny. Bank regulators, who bear the responsibility of safeguarding the stability of the financial system, must understand the impact of these organizations in order to effectively fulfill their duties. This subchapter delves into the pivotal role played by international organizations in shaping financial regulations and the consequences that arise from their actions.

International organizations such as the International Monetary Fund (IMF), the World Bank, and the Financial Stability Board (FSB) have long been at the forefront of efforts to establish and enforce financial regulations. These organizations serve as platforms for collaboration among countries, enabling the exchange of best practices and the development of common regulatory frameworks. By setting standards and guidelines, they assist bank regulators in formulating policies that promote financial stability, transparency, and accountability.

The impact of these organizations on global financial regulations cannot be overstated. Through their initiatives, they strive to address the challenges posed by offshore tax havens, which have been instrumental in facilitating tax evasion and money laundering. By encouraging countries to adopt stricter regulations and cooperate in combating tax avoidance, international organizations have been instrumental in curbing illicit financial activities.

However, the consequences of financial scandals often reverberate beyond tax havens, causing political fallout and resignations. The public outcry stemming from these scandals leads to legal actions and prosecutions, as authorities seek to hold individuals and corporations accountable for their actions. These high-profile cases not only expose social and economic inequalities but also necessitate reforms in corporate transparency and accountability.

Whistleblowers and investigative journalism play a crucial role in uncovering financial wrongdoing, shedding light on the intricate web of corruption and money laundering. International organizations must recognize the significance of whistleblowers and provide them with protection and support to facilitate their invaluable contributions.

The effects of financial scandals extend beyond domestic borders, impacting international relations and diplomacy. These scandals erode public trust and perception of wealth and privilege, fueling resentment and leading to increased scrutiny of the financial sector. Moreover, they have implications for money laundering and corruption, as illicit funds flow across borders, undermining global efforts to combat these criminal activities.

In conclusion, international organizations play a vital role in establishing financial regulations and mitigating the consequences of financial scandals. Bank regulators must work closely with these organizations to develop robust regulatory frameworks that address the challenges posed by offshore tax havens, promote transparency and accountability, and combat money laundering and corruption. By embracing reforms and supporting whistleblowers, international organizations can contribute to restoring public trust, fostering economic stability, and safeguarding the integrity of the global financial system.

International Monetary Fund (IMF)

The International Monetary Fund (IMF) is a global organization that plays a crucial role in maintaining financial stability and promoting economic growth worldwide. Established in 1944, the IMF aims to foster international cooperation, facilitate the expansion and balanced growth of international trade, and provide financial assistance to member countries facing economic difficulties.

Impact on Global Financial Regulations:

The IMF actively participates in shaping global financial regulations by providing guidance and recommendations to member countries. It promotes the adoption of sound economic policies, encourages transparency and accountability, and fosters cooperation among nations to prevent financial crises. The IMF's involvement in global financial regulations has a significant impact on the stability of the banking sector and helps prevent the occurrence of future financial scandals.

Consequences for Offshore Tax Havens:

One of the key areas where the IMF has exerted its influence is in cracking down on offshore tax havens. It has been instrumental in pressuring countries to enhance their tax transparency and curb tax evasion. By promoting the exchange of information and cooperation among tax authorities, the IMF has contributed to reducing the prevalence of tax havens and ensuring a more equitable global tax system.

Political Fallout and Resignations:

Financial scandals often lead to political fallout and high-profile resignations. The IMF closely monitors these developments and assesses their potential impact on global financial stability. It provides guidance to member countries on managing the political fallout and suggests measures to restore public trust in financial institutions.

Legal Actions and Prosecutions:

The IMF supports member countries in their efforts to pursue legal actions and prosecutions against individuals and entities involved in financial scandals. It provides technical assistance, expertise, and financial resources to strengthen legal frameworks and institutions responsible for investigating and prosecuting financial crimes.

Reforms in Corporate Transparency and Accountability:

Financial scandals expose weaknesses in corporate transparency and accountability. The IMF advocates for reforms in corporate governance to enhance transparency, strengthen auditing standards, and improve disclosure requirements. It encourages companies to adopt robust internal control mechanisms and ethical business practices to mitigate the risk of future scandals.

Social and Economic Inequality Exposed:

Financial scandals often highlight the deep-rooted social and economic inequalities within societies. The IMF emphasizes the need for inclusive growth and the reduction of income disparities as a means to prevent future financial crises. It works with member countries to develop policies that promote equitable distribution of resources and enhance social safety nets.

Role of Whistleblowers and Investigative Journalism:

Whistleblowers and investigative journalism play a crucial role in exposing financial scandals. The IMF acknowledges their contribution and advocates for the protection of whistleblowers and the freedom of the press. It supports efforts to strengthen whistleblower protection laws and promotes investigative journalism as a means to uncover corruption and financial wrongdoing.

Effects on International Relations and Diplomacy:

Financial scandals can strain international relations and impact diplomatic ties between countries. The IMF facilitates dialogue and cooperation among nations to address the fallout from financial scandals and restore trust in the global financial system. It encourages countries to work together to implement reforms and strengthen international financial institutions.

Public Perception of Wealth and Privilege:

Financial scandals often lead to a public backlash against the perceived excesses of wealth and privilege. The IMF acknowledges the importance of addressing public concerns and advocates for policies that promote inclusive growth and reduce income inequality. It recognizes the need to restore public trust in financial institutions and ensure that the benefits of economic growth are shared by all.

Implications for Money Laundering and Corruption:

Financial scandals frequently involve money laundering and corruption. The IMF supports member countries in their efforts to combat illicit financial flows, strengthen anti-money laundering measures, and fight against corruption. It provides technical assistance, capacity building, and policy advice to enhance the effectiveness of anti-corruption efforts.

In conclusion, the IMF plays a vital role in addressing the impact of financial scandals on various aspects of the global economy and society. Through its engagement with member countries, the IMF works towards strengthening financial regulations, promoting transparency and accountability, reducing inequality, and restoring public trust in the financial system.

World Bank

The World Bank, an international financial institution, has been at the center of several financial scandals that have had far-reaching implications on global financial regulations. This subchapter will delve into the key controversies surrounding the World Bank and their impact on various aspects of the financial world.

One of the major consequences of these scandals has been the increased scrutiny and regulations on offshore tax havens. As a result of the revelations, bank regulators have tightened their grip on these tax havens, forcing them to disclose more information and comply with stricter regulations.

The political fallout and resignations that followed these scandals shook the global financial community. High-ranking officials and executives were forced to step down amidst public outcry and loss of trust. This led to a wave of legal actions and prosecutions, as governments sought to hold those responsible accountable for their actions.

The scandals also sparked reforms in corporate transparency and accountability. Bank regulators realized the need for stricter regulations and transparency measures to prevent future scandals. This led to the implementation of new policies aimed at enhancing corporate governance and improving accountability within financial institutions.

Moreover, the scandals exposed the stark social and economic inequality that exists in our society. The World Bank's involvement in these controversies shed light on the unjust distribution of wealth and privilege, leading to public outrage and demands for change.

Whistleblowers and investigative journalism played a crucial role in uncovering these scandals. Their bravery in exposing corruption and misconduct within the World Bank was instrumental in initiating legal actions and reforms.

The effects of these scandals extended beyond financial regulations and into international relations and diplomacy. The revelations strained diplomatic ties between countries, as governments demanded answers and sought to protect their national interests.

Public perception of wealth and privilege was significantly impacted by these scandals. The public became more aware of the illicit activities facilitated by offshore tax havens and the corrupt practices within financial institutions. This led to a shift in public opinion and increased pressure on regulators to take action.

Finally, the scandals had profound implications for money laundering and corruption. The exposure of these illicit activities prompted governments to strengthen their anti-money laundering efforts and tighten regulations to combat corruption.

In conclusion, the World Bank scandals had wide-ranging consequences on global financial regulations, offshore tax havens, political landscape, legal actions, corporate transparency, social and economic inequality, whistleblowers, international relations, public perception, and the fight against money laundering and corruption. These controversies underscored the need for stronger regulations and transparency measures within the financial sector and highlighted the importance of holding individuals and institutions accountable for their actions.

Financial Stability Board (FSB)

The Financial Stability Board (FSB) is an international body that plays a crucial role in ensuring global financial stability and protecting the integrity of the financial system. Established in 2009 in response to the global financial crisis, the FSB brings together national authorities, international organizations, and central banks to coordinate and monitor the implementation of effective regulatory, supervisory, and other financial sector policies.

The FSB has had a significant impact on global financial regulations. Through its recommendations and guidelines, the FSB has contributed to the strengthening of regulatory frameworks worldwide. Its focus on identifying and addressing vulnerabilities in the financial system has helped prevent potential crises and promote stability. The FSB's work has also led to increased cooperation among regulators, fostering a more harmonized and consistent approach to financial regulation across different jurisdictions.

One of the consequences of the FSB's efforts has been the scrutiny and crackdown on offshore tax havens. As the FSB emphasizes the importance of transparency and accountability, it has pushed for stricter regulations and measures to combat tax evasion and money laundering. This has forced offshore tax havens to review their practices and implement reforms to meet international standards, reducing the opportunities for illicit financial activities.

The political fallout and resignations resulting from financial scandals have brought the FSB's role into sharp focus. The FSB has been instrumental in identifying regulatory failures and recommending reforms to prevent similar incidents in the future. Its efforts have led to legal actions and prosecutions against individuals and institutions involved in financial misconduct, holding them accountable for their actions.

Reforms in corporate transparency and accountability have been a key focus for the FSB. By promoting the adoption of best practices and standards for corporate governance, the FSB aims to enhance the integrity of the financial system. This includes advocating for improved disclosure of financial information, strengthening risk management practices, and ensuring adequate oversight of executive compensation.

The FSB's work has exposed the social and economic inequality that exists within the financial system. By highlighting the risks and consequences of excessive risk-taking and unethical behavior, the FSB has contributed to a broader conversation about the need for greater fairness and equality in society. This has led to calls for reforms that address the root causes of inequality and promote a more inclusive financial system.

Whistleblowers and investigative journalism have played a crucial role in uncovering financial scandals, and the FSB recognizes their importance. The FSB supports measures to protect whistleblowers and encourages the media to continue their investigative efforts. By shedding light on wrongdoing, whistleblowers and investigative journalists help to hold individuals and institutions accountable and contribute to a more transparent and accountable financial system.

The effects of financial scandals and regulatory failures on international relations and diplomacy cannot be underestimated. They have the potential to strain bilateral and multilateral relationships, eroding trust and cooperation. The FSB's efforts to strengthen global financial stability and restore confidence in the financial system are vital for maintaining positive international relations and facilitating economic growth.

Public perception of wealth and privilege has been profoundly affected by financial scandals. The exposure of unethical practices and the resulting consequences for individuals and institutions involved have led to a heightened awareness of the potential abuses and excesses within the financial sector. This has increased public scrutiny and demand for greater transparency, fairness, and accountability.

The implications for money laundering and corruption have also been significant. The FSB's focus on enhancing regulatory frameworks and promoting international cooperation has played a crucial role in combating these illicit activities. By strengthening anti-money laundering measures and promoting the exchange of information among authorities, the FSB has contributed to making it harder for criminals to exploit the financial system for their illicit gains.

In conclusion, the Financial Stability Board (FSB) has emerged as a key player in safeguarding global financial stability and integrity. Its impact on global financial regulations, consequences for offshore tax havens, and efforts to address political fallout and resignations have helped restore confidence in the financial system. Through legal actions, reforms in corporate transparency, and accountability, and the exposure of social and economic inequality, the FSB has played a significant role in shaping the future of financial governance. The involvement of whistleblowers and investigative journalism, effects on international relations and diplomacy, public perception of wealth and privilege, and implications for money laundering and corruption further highlight the FSB's multifaceted influence on the global financial landscape.

Current Challenges and Loopholes in Global Financial Regulations

In recent years, the global financial system has been rocked by numerous scandals and controversies, exposing significant challenges and loopholes in global financial regulations. This subchapter aims to provide an in-depth analysis of these issues, addressing their impact on various aspects of the financial industry and the consequences they have had on offshore tax havens, political fallout and resignations, legal actions and prosecutions, reforms in corporate transparency and accountability, social and economic inequality, the role of whistleblowers and investigative journalism, effects on international relations and diplomacy, public perception of wealth and privilege, and implications for money laundering and corruption.

One of the major challenges faced by bank regulators is the increasing complexity and sophistication of financial transactions, which has created opportunities for financial institutions and individuals to exploit regulatory gaps. Offshore tax havens, for instance, have become notorious for their role in facilitating tax evasion and money laundering. While efforts have been made to crack down on these havens, their continued existence poses significant challenges to global financial regulations and undermines the integrity of the entire system.

The fallout from financial scandals has also resulted in political repercussions, with high-profile resignations and public outrage over perceived regulatory failures. This has led to a demand for legal actions and prosecutions against those responsible for misconduct. However, the effectiveness of such actions is often hindered by legal loopholes and inadequate international cooperation, which allow wrongdoers to escape accountability.

To address these challenges, reforms in corporate transparency and accountability are imperative. Greater disclosure requirements, enhanced internal controls, and stricter penalties for non-compliance are necessary to restore trust in the financial system. Additionally, social and economic inequality, which has been exposed through these scandals, must be addressed to ensure a fair and equitable financial environment.

The crucial role of whistleblowers and investigative journalism cannot be underestimated in exposing financial wrongdoing. Their courage and determination have played a pivotal role in bringing corrupt practices to light and pushing for regulatory reforms. Protecting whistleblowers and promoting investigative journalism is therefore crucial in maintaining the integrity of global financial regulations.

The consequences of these scandals also extend beyond domestic boundaries, affecting international relations and diplomacy. The revelation of corrupt practices involving foreign entities has strained diplomatic relations and raised concerns about the efficacy of cross-border cooperation in combating financial crimes.

Furthermore, the public perception of wealth and privilege has been significantly impacted by these scandals. The blatant abuse of the financial system by the wealthy and powerful has fueled public outrage and eroded trust in the fairness of the system. This has necessitated a reevaluation of societal values and a critical examination of the concentration of wealth and power.

Finally, the implications for money laundering and corruption cannot be ignored. The exposure of loopholes in global financial regulations has highlighted the need for stronger measures to combat these illicit activities. Strengthened international cooperation, improved regulatory frameworks, and enhanced monitoring mechanisms are essential to prevent further abuse of the financial system.

In conclusion, the current challenges and loopholes in global financial regulations have had far-reaching consequences. Addressing these issues requires a multi-faceted approach that involves reforms in corporate transparency, the protection of whistleblowers, enhanced international cooperation, and a reassessment of societal values. Only through comprehensive and concerted efforts can the integrity of the global financial system be restored and future scandals be prevented.

Chapter 2: Consequences for Offshore Tax Havens

Understanding Offshore Tax Havens

Offshore tax havens have long been a topic of interest and concern in the global financial landscape. These jurisdictions, often small and geographically remote, offer favorable tax benefits and financial secrecy to individuals and corporations seeking to minimize their tax liabilities and protect their assets. However, the impact of offshore tax havens goes far beyond mere tax avoidance. This subchapter aims to shed light on the various dimensions and implications associated with these financial enclaves.

One of the primary concerns surrounding offshore tax havens is their impact on global financial regulations. By providing a safe haven for illicit financial activities, these jurisdictions undermine efforts to establish robust regulatory frameworks. Bank regulators play a crucial role in identifying and addressing these challenges, as they strive to maintain the integrity and stability of the global financial system.

The consequences of offshore tax havens extend beyond regulatory concerns. The prevalence of these havens has led to political fallout and resignations in several instances. High-ranking officials and public figures have faced scrutiny and public backlash for their involvement in offshore tax schemes, often resulting in their resignation or forced departure from office. These scandals have eroded public trust and highlighted the need for stronger legal actions and prosecutions against those involved.

In response to the growing outcry, reforms in corporate transparency and accountability have been proposed. The offshore world operates in secrecy, enabling fraudulent activities and facilitating money laundering and corruption. By enhancing transparency and holding corporations accountable for their actions, regulators aim to minimize the risks posed by offshore tax havens.

The exposure of social and economic inequality has been another consequence of offshore tax havens. These havens have allowed the wealthy elite to amass vast fortunes while evading their fair share of taxes. This disparity has intensified public resentment and has ignited debates about wealth distribution and social justice.

Whistleblowers and investigative journalism have played a crucial role in uncovering the inner workings of offshore tax havens. These individuals and organizations have brought to light the extent of corruption and illicit financial activities, forcing governments and regulators to take action. Their role in exposing the truth and holding the powerful accountable cannot be overstated.

The effects of offshore tax havens also extend beyond domestic borders, impacting international relations and diplomacy. Countries have engaged in diplomatic negotiations and agreements to combat tax evasion and promote tax transparency. These efforts have reshaped the dynamics of global cooperation and have emphasized the need for collaborative action in addressing cross-border financial crimes.

Furthermore, the public perception of wealth and privilege has been significantly influenced by offshore tax havens. These havens have perpetuated the notion of a global elite that operates outside the bounds of national laws and regulations. As a result, public sentiment towards the wealthy has shifted, with a growing demand for greater accountability and fairness.

Lastly, the implications for money laundering and corruption cannot be ignored. Offshore tax havens provide a fertile ground for illicit financial flows, enabling criminals to conceal their ill-gotten gains. This subchapter will explore the link between offshore tax havens and money laundering, highlighting the necessity for stringent measures to combat these illicit activities.

Overall, understanding offshore tax havens is crucial for bank regulators as they strive to protect the integrity and stability of the global financial system. The subchapter will delve into the multifaceted dimensions of offshore tax havens, exploring their impact on global financial regulations, consequences for these jurisdictions, political fallout and resignations, legal actions and prosecutions, reforms in corporate transparency and accountability, social and economic inequality, the role of whistleblowers and investigative journalism, effects on international relations and diplomacy, public perception of wealth and privilege, and implications for money laundering and corruption.

Role of Offshore Tax Havens in Financial Scandals

Subchapter: Role of Offshore Tax Havens in Financial Scandals

Introduction:

The role of offshore tax havens in financial scandals has been a subject of significant concern and scrutiny in recent years. This subchapter aims to provide bank regulators with an in-depth understanding of the impact of offshore tax havens on global financial regulations, the consequences associated with their usage, and the implications for various aspects of society and the economy.

Impact on Global Financial Regulations:

Offshore tax havens have played a detrimental role in undermining global financial regulations. By providing a safe haven for illicit financial activities, these jurisdictions have made it easier for individuals and corporations to evade taxes, engage in money laundering, and hide their wealth. This subversion of regulations has weakened the integrity of the global financial system and hindered efforts to combat financial crimes.

Consequences for Offshore Tax Havens:

The consequences of offshore tax havens extend beyond the realm of financial regulations. These jurisdictions often suffer from reputational damage due to their association with financial scandals. International organizations and governments have imposed sanctions and restrictions on these havens, leading to a loss of business and investment opportunities. Moreover, their economies heavily rely on the revenue generated from offshore financial services, and any decline in their reputation can have severe economic consequences.

Political Fallout and Resignations:

Financial scandals involving offshore tax havens have frequently led to political fallout and high-profile resignations. Public outrage over the involvement of politicians and government officials in illicit activities has resulted in calls for accountability and transparency. The exposure of corruption and unethical practices has eroded public trust in political institutions and fueled demands for political reform.

Legal Actions and Prosecutions:

The revelation of financial scandals often triggers legal actions and prosecutions against those involved. Authorities have increasingly focused on investigating and prosecuting individuals and corporations utilizing offshore tax havens for illegal purposes. These legal actions serve as a deterrent and send a clear message that financial crimes will not go unpunished.

Reforms in Corporate Transparency and Accountability:

Financial scandals have prompted a wave of reforms in corporate transparency and accountability. Governments and regulatory bodies have introduced stricter regulations and disclosure requirements to prevent the misuse of offshore tax havens. Companies are now expected to provide detailed information regarding their offshore activities, ensuring greater transparency and reducing the potential for illicit financial practices.

Social and Economic Inequality Exposed:

The use of offshore tax havens has further exposed the social and economic inequality prevalent in society. These havens enable the wealthy elite to accumulate vast amounts of wealth while evading their fair share of taxes. As a result, the burden of taxation falls disproportionately on the middle and lower classes, exacerbating existing inequalities and hindering social progress.

Role of Whistleblowers and Investigative Journalism:

Whistleblowers and investigative journalists have played a crucial role in uncovering financial scandals involving offshore tax havens. Their brave efforts have exposed the illicit activities of individuals and corporations, leading to public awareness, legal actions, and reforms. Their contributions highlight the importance of protecting whistleblowers and supporting investigative journalism in the fight against financial crimes.

Effects on International Relations and Diplomacy:

Financial scandals involving offshore tax havens can strain international relations and diplomacy. Countries may retaliate against havens that facilitate illicit financial activities, leading to tensions and conflicts. Additionally, the cooperation between nations in combating financial crimes becomes crucial, highlighting the need for enhanced international collaboration and information sharing.

Public Perception of Wealth and Privilege:

Financial scandals have significantly impacted public perception regarding wealth and privilege. The exposure of high-profile individuals and corporations engaging in illegal activities has fueled public anger and resentment towards the wealthy elite. This has resulted in increased demands for fairness, equality, and a reevaluation of societal values.

Implications for Money Laundering and Corruption:

Offshore tax havens have become hotspots for money laundering and corruption due to their secretive nature and lax regulations. Financial scandals have shed light on the extent of these illicit activities, necessitating a comprehensive approach to combat money laundering and corruption. Strengthening international cooperation and implementing stringent measures are essential to tackling these issues effectively.

Conclusion:

The role of offshore tax havens in financial scandals has had far-reaching consequences across various sectors. Bank regulators must recognize the detrimental impact these havens have on global financial regulations, the economy, politics, and society as a whole. Efforts to address these issues should encompass legal actions, reforms, transparency, accountability, and international cooperation to restore trust in the financial system and create a level playing field for all stakeholders.

Impact on Tax Revenues and Economic Development

In the wake of financial scandals and the subsequent political fallout and resignations, the impact on tax revenues and economic development cannot be ignored. This subchapter delves into the profound consequences these scandals have had on global financial regulations, offshore tax havens, legal actions and prosecutions, corporate transparency and accountability, social and economic inequality, and much more.

One of the immediate effects of financial scandals is the erosion of tax revenues. As individuals and corporations engage in fraudulent activities, they exploit loopholes in tax laws and engage in aggressive tax planning, depriving governments of much-needed funds. This, in turn, affects economic development as governments struggle to provide public goods and services, invest in infrastructure, and foster economic growth. The impact is particularly severe in developing countries, where the diversion of funds exacerbates poverty and hampers progress.

Furthermore, financial scandals expose the vulnerabilities of offshore tax havens. These havens, often characterized by lax regulations and secrecy, attract illicit flows of capital, facilitating tax evasion and money laundering. As the scandals unfold, regulatory bodies are compelled to reevaluate their oversight of these tax havens, leading to stricter regulations and increased scrutiny. The consequences for offshore tax havens are significant, as they face reputational damage and decreased attractiveness for individuals and corporations seeking to hide their assets and avoid taxes.

Legal actions and prosecutions play a crucial role in restoring faith in the financial system. As the scandals unfold, law enforcement agencies, in cooperation with regulatory bodies, initiate investigations and bring the perpetrators to justice. Prosecutions not only serve as a deterrent but also signal a commitment to upholding the rule of law. The success of these legal actions and prosecutions depends on the effectiveness of regulatory bodies, cooperation between jurisdictions, and the availability of evidence.

Financial scandals also prompt reforms in corporate transparency and accountability. The public demand for increased transparency and accountability forces companies to disclose more information regarding their financial activities. Regulatory bodies respond by implementing stricter reporting requirements and enhancing corporate governance frameworks. These reforms aim to restore trust in the corporate sector and ensure that executives and board members act in the best interest of shareholders and stakeholders.

Moreover, financial scandals expose the stark reality of social and economic inequality. As the scandals unravel, the public becomes acutely aware of the disparities between the wealthy elites and the rest of society. This awareness fuels public outrage and demands for greater equality and fairness. Governments, under pressure from public sentiment, may introduce policies aimed at reducing inequality, such as progressive taxation, wealth redistribution, and investments in social programs.

The role of whistleblowers and investigative journalism cannot be overstated in uncovering financial scandals. Whistleblowers, driven by a sense of justice or self-interest, provide critical information to regulatory bodies and the media, exposing wrongdoing and initiating investigations. Investigative journalism supports these efforts by conducting in-depth research, revealing hidden connections, and shedding light on the inner workings of financial scandals. Both whistleblowers and investigative journalists play a vital role in holding individuals and institutions accountable.

On the international stage, financial scandals have far-reaching effects on international relations and diplomacy. As scandals implicate individuals and corporations from different countries, cooperation between jurisdictions becomes essential. Governments must collaborate to share information, freeze assets, and prosecute offenders.

These collaborations can strain diplomatic relations, particularly when powerful actors are involved. However, effective cooperation is crucial to ensure the stability and integrity of the global financial system.

Moreover, financial scandals affect public perception of wealth and privilege. As the scandals unfold, the public becomes disillusioned with the wealthy elites who manipulate the system to their advantage. This perception shift can lead to a loss of faith in traditional institutions and a rise in populist movements. The consequences of this public sentiment can be unpredictable but may include increased scrutiny of the wealthy, calls for wealth redistribution, and demands for systemic reforms.

Lastly, financial scandals have significant implications for money laundering and corruption. As investigations progress, the web of illegal activities often extends beyond tax evasion, revealing money laundering operations and corrupt practices. Governments and regulatory bodies must strengthen their anti-money laundering efforts, enhance due diligence procedures, and improve surveillance mechanisms. These actions aim to prevent illicit funds from entering the financial system and ensure the integrity of financial transactions.

In conclusion, financial scandals have a profound impact on tax revenues and economic development. They expose vulnerabilities in global financial regulations, challenge the viability of offshore tax havens, initiate legal actions and prosecutions, prompt reforms in corporate transparency and accountability, shed light on social and economic inequality, highlight the role of whistleblowers and investigative journalism, affect international relations and diplomacy, shape public perception of wealth and privilege, and emphasize the need to combat money laundering and corruption. Addressing these issues is crucial for restoring trust in the financial system, fostering economic development, and promoting a fair and just society.

International Efforts to Combat Offshore Tax Havens

In recent years, the issue of offshore tax havens has gained significant attention due to their impact on global financial regulations and the consequences they pose for the global economy. This subchapter delves into the international efforts made to combat these tax havens, addressing their political fallout, legal actions, and the subsequent reforms in corporate transparency and accountability.

Offshore tax havens have long been a safe haven for the world's wealthiest individuals and corporations seeking to minimize their tax obligations. However, the detrimental effects of these havens on the global economy cannot be overlooked. Recognizing this, international organizations such as the Organization for Economic Cooperation and Development (OECD) and the Financial Action Task Force (FATF) have taken significant steps to combat offshore tax evasion.

These efforts have resulted in a wave of political fallout and resignations, as the public becomes increasingly aware of the extent to which their leaders and corporations exploit these havens. The Panama Papers scandal, for instance, exposed the involvement of numerous politicians, celebrities, and corporations in offshore tax evasion, leading to widespread public outrage and demands for accountability.

In response to these revelations, governments worldwide have initiated legal actions and prosecutions against individuals and entities involved in offshore tax evasion. High-profile cases have resulted in hefty fines, imprisonment, and even the seizure of assets. These legal actions send a clear message that tax evasion will not be tolerated, further deterring individuals and corporations from using tax havens.

To prevent future occurrences, reforms in corporate transparency and accountability have become a priority. Governments have implemented measures such as the Common Reporting Standard

(CRS), which requires financial institutions to share information about their clients' offshore accounts with relevant tax authorities. These reforms aim to close loopholes and ensure that individuals and corporations are held accountable for their tax obligations.

The exposure of offshore tax havens has also shed light on the social and economic inequality that plagues societies worldwide. The public has become increasingly aware of the vast wealth hidden away in these havens, exacerbating the divide between the rich and the poor. This heightened awareness has sparked discussions and debates on the need for a fairer tax system and the redistribution of wealth.

The role of whistleblowers and investigative journalism cannot be underestimated in bringing these offshore tax havens to light. Whistleblowers such as Edward Snowden and journalists working on projects like the Panama Papers have played a crucial role in uncovering the extent of tax evasion and corruption. Their courage and dedication have led to greater transparency and accountability in the global financial system.

The effects of offshore tax havens extend beyond domestic borders, impacting international relations and diplomacy. Countries that shelter tax evaders face increased scrutiny and pressure from other nations to crack down on these illicit activities. As a result, diplomatic relations may suffer, and international cooperation in fighting tax evasion is emphasized.

The public perception of wealth and privilege has also been affected by the exposure of offshore tax havens. The revelation that the wealthiest individuals and corporations can avoid paying their fair share of taxes has fueled public anger and distrust. Consequently, the public demands greater accountability and fairness in the tax system.

In conclusion, international efforts to combat offshore tax havens have gained momentum in recent years. The political fallout, legal actions, and subsequent reforms in corporate transparency and accountability have exposed the social and economic inequality perpetuated by these tax havens. Whistleblowers and investigative journalism have played a crucial role in bringing these issues to light. As the world becomes more interconnected, the implications of offshore tax havens on global financial regulations, money laundering, corruption, and international relations cannot be ignored. The fight against offshore tax evasion continues, with the aim of creating a fairer and more transparent global financial system.

The Organization for Economic Co-operation and Development (OECD)

The Organization for Economic Co-operation and Development (OECD) is an international organization that promotes economic growth, stability, and improved living standards for its member countries. Established in 1961, the OECD serves as a platform for governments to discuss and coordinate economic policies, share best practices, and address global challenges.

Impact on Global Financial Regulations:

The OECD plays a crucial role in shaping global financial regulations. Through its various committees and working groups, the organization develops and promotes international standards and guidelines to ensure transparency, integrity, and accountability in the financial sector. Its recommendations on topics such as tax evasion, money laundering, and corporate governance have a significant impact on regulatory frameworks worldwide.

Consequences for Offshore Tax Havens:

One of the key areas the OECD addresses is the issue of offshore tax havens. By working closely with member countries, the organization has been successful in cracking down on tax avoidance and evasion schemes. It has developed the Common Reporting Standard (CRS) to facilitate the automatic exchange of financial information between countries, making it harder for individuals and businesses to hide their assets offshore.

Political Fallout and Resignations:

Financial scandals often lead to political fallout and resignations. The OECD closely monitors these developments and calls for accountability and transparency in government and financial institutions. By exposing corrupt practices and advocating for legal actions, the organization seeks to restore public trust and ensure that those responsible for the scandals face appropriate consequences.

Legal Actions and Prosecutions:

The OECD actively supports member countries in their efforts to prosecute individuals and corporations involved in financial misconduct. It provides a platform for sharing information and coordinating international legal actions against offenders. Through its Anti-Bribery Convention, the OECD has been instrumental in fighting corruption and bribery in both the public and private sectors.

Reforms in Corporate Transparency and Accountability:

Financial scandals often reveal the need for reforms in corporate transparency and accountability. The OECD develops guidelines and recommendations to enhance corporate governance practices, strengthen internal controls, and promote responsible business conduct. Its efforts aim to prevent future scandals by fostering a culture of transparency and ethical behavior within corporations.

Social and Economic Inequality Exposed:

Financial scandals often highlight the growing social and economic inequality within societies. The OECD recognizes this issue and advocates for policies that promote inclusive growth and reduce inequality. By analyzing the root causes of financial scandals, the organization provides insights into the broader societal challenges that need to be addressed.

Role of Whistleblowers and Investigative Journalism:

Whistleblowers and investigative journalism play a vital role in exposing financial scandals. The OECD acknowledges their contribution and works to protect whistleblowers, encourage their disclosures, and ensure their information leads to appropriate actions and reforms. The organization also collaborates with journalists and media organizations to raise awareness about financial misconduct and its consequences.

Effects on International Relations and Diplomacy:

Financial scandals can strain international relations and diplomacy. The OECD facilitates dialogue and cooperation between member countries to address the cross-border implications of financial misconduct. By fostering trust and collaboration, the organization aims to prevent conflicts and promote a harmonized global response to financial scandals.

Public Perception of Wealth and Privilege:

Financial scandals often lead to a shift in public perception regarding wealth and privilege. The OECD recognizes the need to address this perception and works to promote fairness, equal opportunities, and social mobility. Through its policies and initiatives, the organization aims to restore public trust in the financial system and ensure that wealth is generated and distributed in a more equitable manner.

Implications for Money Laundering and Corruption:

Financial scandals are closely linked to money laundering and corruption. The OECD provides guidance and support to member countries in their efforts to combat these illegal activities. By developing international standards, promoting information exchange, and assisting in capacity building, the organization helps strengthen anti-money laundering and anti-corruption measures globally.

In conclusion, the Organization for Economic Co-operation and Development (OECD) plays a crucial role in addressing the impact of financial scandals. Its work on global financial regulations, offshore tax havens, political fallout, legal actions, corporate transparency, social and economic inequality, whistleblowers, international relations, public perception, and money laundering and corruption have far-reaching implications for bank regulators and the wider financial community. By promoting transparency, accountability, and responsible conduct, the OECD aims to prevent future financial scandals and foster sustainable economic growth.

Common Reporting Standard (CRS)

The Common Reporting Standard (CRS) is a global initiative aimed at combating tax evasion and promoting financial transparency. Developed by the Organisation for Economic Co-operation and Development (OECD), the CRS sets out a comprehensive framework for the automatic exchange of financial information between countries.

Impact on Global Financial Regulations:

The implementation of CRS has had a significant impact on global financial regulations. It has led to a shift towards greater transparency and cooperation between jurisdictions, as countries are now required to exchange financial information on a regular basis. This has helped in uncovering hidden assets, identifying tax evaders, and preventing illicit financial flows.

Consequences for Offshore Tax Havens:

Offshore tax havens have long been associated with tax evasion and money laundering. The CRS has made it increasingly difficult for individuals and corporations to hide their wealth in these jurisdictions. With the automatic exchange of financial information, tax authorities now have access to a wealth of data that can be used to identify and pursue tax evaders.

Political Fallout and Resignations:

The implementation of CRS has not been without its share of political fallout. Several high-profile individuals and politicians have been implicated in financial scandals as a result of the increased transparency brought about by CRS. This has led to public outrage and calls for greater accountability in the political sphere, resulting in resignations and changes in leadership.

Legal Actions and Prosecutions:

The exposure of financial wrongdoing through CRS has led to an increase in legal actions and prosecutions. Tax evaders and those involved in money laundering and corruption are being held accountable for their actions. This has served as a deterrent and has helped in restoring public trust in the financial system.

Reforms in Corporate Transparency and Accountability:

The implementation of CRS has also resulted in significant reforms in corporate transparency and accountability. Companies are now required to disclose their beneficial ownership structures, making it harder for them to engage in illicit activities. This has promoted fair competition and improved corporate governance.

Social and Economic Inequality Exposed:

CRS has shed light on the extent of social and economic inequality by revealing the vast wealth held in offshore accounts. The disparity between the rich and the poor has become more apparent, leading to calls for wealth redistribution and increased taxation on the wealthiest individuals.

Role of Whistleblowers and Investigative Journalism:

Whistleblowers and investigative journalism have played a crucial role in uncovering financial scandals exposed by CRS. Their efforts have brought hidden information to light and have been instrumental in holding individuals and institutions accountable for their actions.

Effects on International Relations and Diplomacy:

The implementation of CRS has had a profound impact on international relations and diplomacy. Countries that have been identified as tax havens or facilitators of tax evasion have faced increased scrutiny and pressure from the international community. This has led to diplomatic tensions and a reevaluation of bilateral relationships.

Public Perception of Wealth and Privilege:

The exposure of offshore accounts and tax evasion schemes has changed the public perception of wealth and privilege. There is now a greater awareness of the unfair advantages enjoyed by the wealthy and the need for a more equitable distribution of resources.

Implications for Money Laundering and Corruption:

CRS has had significant implications for money laundering and corruption. The automatic exchange of financial information has made it more difficult for illicit funds to be moved across borders undetected. This has disrupted criminal networks and reduced opportunities for corruption.

In conclusion, the implementation of CRS has had far-reaching implications for global financial regulations, offshore tax havens, political systems, legal actions, corporate transparency, social and economic inequality, whistleblowers, international relations, public perception, and money laundering. It has brought about a paradigm shift in the way financial transactions are conducted and has paved the way for a more transparent and accountable financial system.

Evaluating the Effectiveness of Measures Against Offshore Tax Havens

Offshore tax havens have long been a subject of controversy and concern for bank regulators worldwide. These financial jurisdictions, known for their low tax rates, lax regulations, and secretive banking practices, have often been associated with illicit financial activities, including tax evasion, money laundering, and corruption. In this subchapter, we will delve into the effectiveness of measures taken against offshore tax havens and their impact on various aspects of the global financial landscape.

The consequences for offshore tax havens have been significant in recent years. Governments and regulatory bodies have been actively pursuing legal actions and prosecutions against individuals and corporations involved in offshore tax evasion. These efforts have resulted in high-profile resignations and political fallout as public outrage over financial scandals grows. The exposure of social and economic inequality, with the privileged few evading taxes while the majority suffers, has further fueled public discontent.

One of the key factors in uncovering offshore tax havens' activities has been the role of whistleblowers and investigative journalism. These actors have played a crucial role in shedding light on the hidden financial dealings and exposing the lack of transparency and accountability in offshore jurisdictions. Their efforts have not only triggered legal actions but also brought about reforms in corporate transparency and accountability, forcing offshore tax havens to adopt stricter regulations.

The effects on international relations and diplomacy cannot be underestimated. The revelation of individuals and entities using offshore tax havens to hide wealth and evade taxes has strained diplomatic ties between countries. Governments have been pressured to cooperate and share information to combat tax evasion and money laundering effectively. As a result, international agreements and initiatives have been established to promote cooperation and information exchange, such as the Common Reporting Standard and the Automatic Exchange of Financial Account Information.

Furthermore, the public perception of wealth and privilege has been significantly impacted by the exposure of offshore tax havens. The revelation that the ultra-wealthy can exploit legal loopholes to avoid taxation has led to increased scrutiny and demands for fairer wealth distribution. The notion of social responsibility among corporations and individuals has gained prominence, and public sentiment has shifted towards a stronger stance against tax avoidance and evasion.

In conclusion, the measures taken against offshore tax havens have brought significant changes to the global financial regulations. The political fallout and resignations resulting from financial scandals have highlighted the urgency for reform and accountability. Legal actions and prosecutions have sent a strong message that offshore tax evasion will not be tolerated. Reforms in corporate transparency and accountability have been implemented, and the role of whistleblowers and investigative journalism in exposing financial wrongdoing has been acknowledged. The impact on international relations, public perception, money laundering, and corruption has been profound. However, continuous evaluation and adaptation of these measures will be necessary to ensure the effectiveness of efforts against offshore tax havens and to safeguard the integrity of the global financial system.

Chapter 3: Political Fallout and Resignations

Political Consequences of Financial Scandals

Financial scandals have far-reaching political consequences that extend beyond the immediate economic impact. This subchapter explores the various ways in which financial scandals can shape political landscapes, influence global financial regulations, and lead to significant political fallout and resignations.

One of the key consequences of financial scandals is their impact on global financial regulations. When high-profile scandals occur, regulators are often compelled to review and tighten regulations to prevent similar incidents in the future. These scandals expose loopholes and weaknesses in existing regulatory frameworks, prompting regulators to reassess and strengthen their oversight of financial institutions. Bank regulators must stay abreast of these developments to adapt their strategies and ensure that they are effectively monitoring the industry.

Financial scandals also have consequences for offshore tax havens. These scandals reveal the extent to which individuals and corporations exploit offshore tax havens to evade taxes and engage in illicit financial activities. As a result, pressure mounts on regulators to crack down on these havens, leading to increased scrutiny and calls for greater transparency in international financial transactions.

Moreover, financial scandals often trigger political fallout and resignations. Public trust in government institutions and financial regulators can be severely eroded when scandals occur under their watch. Politicians and regulators may face public outrage and demands for accountability, which can ultimately result in resignations, dismissals, or even changes in government leadership. Bank regulators must be prepared to navigate these politically charged situations and ensure that the necessary actions are taken to restore public trust.

Legal actions and prosecutions are another consequence of financial scandals. When wrongdoing is uncovered, regulators and law enforcement agencies are tasked with holding individuals and corporations accountable. Bank regulators play a crucial role in assisting with investigations, providing evidence, and cooperating with legal authorities to ensure that justice is served.

Reforms in corporate transparency and accountability are often prompted by financial scandals. Scandals expose the lack of transparency and accountability within corporations, leading to public demands for stricter regulations and greater corporate responsibility. Bank regulators must support and enforce these reforms to enhance the integrity of the financial system.

Financial scandals also shed light on social and economic inequality. They reveal the extent to which wealth and privilege can be used to manipulate the system, exacerbating existing social and economic disparities. These revelations can fuel public discontent and calls for greater equality and fairness in society.

The role of whistleblowers and investigative journalism in uncovering financial scandals cannot be underestimated. Whistleblowers play a critical role in exposing wrongdoing, and investigative journalists play a vital role in bringing these scandals to light. Bank regulators should encourage and protect whistleblowers, as well as collaborate with journalists, to ensure that financial wrongdoing is exposed and addressed.

Financial scandals can also have implications for international relations and diplomacy. When scandals involve multinational corporations or individuals with ties to foreign governments, it can strain diplomatic relations and create tensions between countries. Bank regulators must be aware of these implications and collaborate with international counterparts to address cross-border financial misconduct.

Furthermore, financial scandals can shape public perception of wealth and privilege. Scandals involving extravagant spending, fraud, and corruption can lead to a negative perception of the wealthy and privileged. This can have political ramifications and influence public opinion on issues such as taxation and income inequality.

Finally, financial scandals have implications for money laundering and corruption. They expose the vulnerabilities within the financial system that allow illicit funds to be laundered and corrupt practices to flourish. Bank regulators must work to strengthen anti-money laundering measures and enforce strict regulations to prevent further abuse of the financial system.

In conclusion, financial scandals have profound political consequences that impact global financial regulations, offshore tax havens, political stability, corporate transparency, social and economic inequality, international relations, public perception, and the fight against money laundering and corruption. Bank regulators must be attuned to these consequences and adapt their strategies and oversight to address the fallout from financial scandals effectively.

Loss of Public Trust and Confidence

In the aftermath of financial scandals, one of the most significant consequences is the loss of public trust and confidence in the banking industry. The revelations of widespread corruption, money laundering, and tax evasion erode the belief that banks are reliable institutions that can be trusted with people's hard-earned money. This loss of trust has far-reaching implications for the global financial system and necessitates urgent action from bank regulators.

The impact on global financial regulations cannot be overstated. As the public becomes disillusioned with the banking sector, there is an increasing demand for stricter regulations to prevent such scandals from occurring again. Regulators must respond by implementing robust frameworks that promote transparency, accountability, and ethical behavior. The need for international cooperation to combat offshore tax havens also becomes evident, as these havens contribute to the erosion of public trust.

The political fallout and resignations that follow financial scandals are inevitable. The public demands accountability from politicians who may have turned a blind eye or actively participated in these illegal activities. The resignation of key figures in both the banking and political sectors is not only a consequence of public pressure but also an opportunity for change. New leadership must be appointed to restore public confidence and implement reforms.

Legal action and prosecutions against those involved in financial scandals are essential to rebuilding trust. The public expects justice to be served and for those responsible to face the consequences of their actions. Regulators must work closely with law enforcement agencies to ensure that individuals are held accountable, regardless of their wealth or social status.

Reforms in corporate transparency and accountability are crucial in restoring public trust. Banks must be more transparent about their operations and financial transactions. This includes disclosing information about offshore tax havens, beneficial ownership, and money flows. Strengthening corporate governance and ensuring effective oversight mechanisms will help prevent future scandals.

Financial scandals often expose the social and economic inequalities that exist within society. The public becomes more aware of the privileges enjoyed by the wealthy and the extent to which they can manipulate the system for personal gain. This exposure fuels public anger and calls for a fairer distribution of wealth and resources.

Whistleblowers and investigative journalism play a vital role in bringing financial scandals to light. Their courage and dedication in exposing wrongdoing help to restore faith in the system. Regulators must protect whistleblowers and encourage investigative journalism as a means to hold banks accountable.

The effects of financial scandals on international relations and diplomacy cannot be ignored. These scandals strain relationships between countries, particularly when tax evasion and money laundering involve offshore havens. Cooperation between nations becomes essential in combating these issues and restoring trust in the global financial system.

Public perception of wealth and privilege is significantly impacted by financial scandals. The image of the wealthy elite as untouchable and immune to the consequences of their actions is shattered. The public demands fairness and equal treatment under the law.

Finally, financial scandals have severe implications for money laundering and corruption. The public's trust in the financial system is undermined when banks are found to be facilitating illegal activities. Regulators must strengthen anti-money laundering measures and enforce strict penalties to deter such behavior.

In conclusion, the loss of public trust and confidence resulting from financial scandals has profound implications for the banking industry and the global financial system. Bank regulators must take swift and decisive action to restore trust, implement reforms, and hold those responsible accountable. Only through these measures can the industry regain the public's confidence and prevent future scandals.

Resignations and Political Fallout

In the realm of financial scandals, resignations and political fallout are inevitable consequences that can have far-reaching implications. This subchapter delves into the aftermath of such events, shedding light on the various dimensions and impacts they have on global financial regulations, offshore tax havens, legal actions, corporate transparency, social and economic inequality, whistleblowers, international relations, public perception, and the fight against money laundering and corruption.

When a financial scandal erupts, it often exposes the weaknesses and loopholes in existing global financial regulations. Bank regulators must closely examine these incidents to identify the gaps and improve regulatory frameworks to prevent similar occurrences in the future. The resignation of high-ranking officials and the subsequent political fallout can act as a catalyst for regulatory reforms, leading to stricter oversight and enhanced transparency measures.

Offshore tax havens, notorious for facilitating illicit financial activities and allowing individuals and corporations to evade taxes, are particularly affected by resignations and political fallout. These events prompt intensified scrutiny and calls for cracking down on these havens, leading to increased cooperation among nations to tackle tax evasion and money laundering.

Resignations and political fallout often trigger legal actions and prosecutions against those involved in financial scandals. In the pursuit of justice, the legal system plays a crucial role in holding individuals and corporations accountable for their actions. These legal proceedings serve as a deterrent and send a strong message that financial misconduct will not be tolerated.

Corporate transparency and accountability are closely linked to resignations and political fallout. These events expose the shortcomings in corporate governance practices, prompting demands for reforms that ensure greater transparency, accountability, and ethical behavior in the corporate world. This, in turn, helps restore public trust and confidence in the financial system.

Financial scandals often shed light on the deep-seated social and economic inequalities that exist within societies. The exposure of corrupt practices and the subsequent fallout highlight the stark contrast between the privileged few and the majority struggling to make ends meet. Such revelations can fuel public outrage and mobilize efforts to address these inequalities, both within the financial sector and society at large.

Whistleblowers and investigative journalism play a pivotal role in uncovering financial scandals. Their courage and determination to unearth the truth can lead to resignations, public investigations, and political consequences. Recognizing the importance of whistleblowers and supporting investigative journalism is crucial for maintaining a transparent and accountable financial system.

The political fallout and resignations resulting from financial scandals can have significant effects on international relations and diplomacy. These events can strain diplomatic ties and cooperation between nations, particularly when offshore tax havens or illicit funds are involved. It is therefore imperative for countries to address these issues in a collaborative manner, fostering trust and cooperation in combating financial misconduct.

Public perception of wealth and privilege is profoundly influenced by the fallout from financial scandals. These events can expose the excesses and unethical practices of the wealthy elite, leading to public disillusionment and a demand for a more equitable society. Resignations and political consequences can serve as a wake-up call for societies to reevaluate their values and priorities.

Lastly, resignations and political fallout have direct implications for the fight against money laundering and corruption. By exposing the inner workings of illicit financial activities, these events help authorities identify vulnerabilities and strengthen anti-money laundering measures. They also send a clear message to corrupt actors that their actions will not go unpunished.

In conclusion, resignations and political fallout resulting from financial scandals have wide-ranging impacts on various aspects of society and the global financial system. From regulatory reforms to international cooperation, from legal actions to social change, these events shape the future of financial regulations, corporate transparency, public perception, and the fight against inequality, money laundering, and corruption. Bank regulators must closely examine these consequences and take proactive measures to prevent and mitigate such scandals in the future.

Case Studies: Notable Resignations and Political Fallout

In this subchapter, we will delve into a number of notable resignations and the political fallout that ensued as a consequence of financial scandals. These case studies shed light on the intricate web of corruption, money laundering, and regulatory failures that have plagued the global financial system. Bank regulators will gain valuable insights into the impact on global financial regulations, consequences for offshore tax havens, political fallout and resignations, legal actions and prosecutions, reforms in corporate transparency and accountability, social and economic inequality exposed, the role of whistleblowers and investigative journalism, effects on international relations and diplomacy, public perception of wealth and privilege, and implications for money laundering and corruption.

One such case study involves the high-profile resignation of a prominent banking executive who was accused of orchestrating a large-scale money laundering operation through offshore tax havens. This scandal not only exposed the loopholes and weaknesses in global financial regulations but also sparked a political firestorm, leading to the resignation of several government officials who were implicated in the scandal. Bank regulators will gain insights into the specific regulatory failures that allowed such a massive operation to go undetected, as well as the subsequent reforms in corporate transparency and accountability that were implemented to prevent similar incidents in the future.

Another case study focuses on the role of whistleblowers and investigative journalism in uncovering financial scandals and forcing resignations. Through their courageous actions, whistleblowers exposed deep-rooted corruption and illicit activities within powerful financial institutions, leading to the downfall of influential figures. This case study highlights the importance of protecting and incentivizing whistleblowers, as well as the critical role that investigative journalism plays in holding the powerful accountable.

Furthermore, we will explore the implications of financial scandals on international relations and diplomacy. These scandals often involve cross-border transactions and illicit funds flowing through offshore tax havens, which can strain diplomatic relations between countries. Bank regulators will gain insights into the challenges faced in coordinating international efforts to combat money laundering and corruption while preserving diplomatic ties.

Overall, this subchapter will provide bank regulators with a comprehensive understanding of the notable resignations and political fallout resulting from financial scandals. By studying these case studies, regulators can identify the loopholes in global financial regulations, implement necessary reforms, and strengthen efforts to combat corruption, money laundering, and social and economic inequality.

Watergate Scandal: Richard Nixon's Resignation

The Watergate Scandal, marked by the resignation of President Richard Nixon, remains one of the most significant events in modern American political history. Its impact on global financial regulations, consequences for offshore tax havens, political fallout and resignations, legal actions and prosecutions, reforms in corporate transparency and accountability, social and economic inequality exposed, role of whistleblowers and investigative journalism, effects on international relations and diplomacy, public perception of wealth and privilege, and implications for money laundering and corruption cannot be understated.

The Watergate Scandal began with a break-in at the Democratic National Committee headquarters in 1972, orchestrated by individuals connected to Nixon's administration. As the scandal unraveled, it became clear that Nixon had been involved in a cover-up, attempting to obstruct justice and abuse the powers of his office. The subsequent investigations and hearings led to a series of revelations that shook the foundations of American democracy.

The scandal had far-reaching implications for global financial regulations. As the world watched the downfall of a powerful leader, it exposed the vulnerabilities and risks associated with offshore tax havens. The Watergate Scandal served as a wake-up call for bank regulators, highlighting the need for stricter oversight and regulations to prevent financial crimes and corruption.

The political fallout and resignations resulting from the Watergate Scandal were unprecedented. Nixon's resignation in 1974 marked a turning point in American politics, eroding public trust and confidence in government institutions. The scandal led to a wave of legal actions and prosecutions, holding individuals accountable for their involvement in the cover-up. This sent a clear message that no one is above the law, regardless of their position or influence.

Reforms in corporate transparency and accountability became imperative in the aftermath of Watergate. The scandal exposed the dark underbelly of corporate power and the potential for abuse. As a result, regulations were put in place to ensure greater transparency in corporate practices, safeguarding against corruption and unethical behavior.

The Watergate Scandal also shed light on social and economic inequality, as it exposed the close ties between political elites and the privileged class. The scandal fueled public outrage and a growing sense of distrust towards the wealthy and powerful. This perception shift had a lasting impact on the public's perception of wealth and privilege, reinforcing the need for a fairer and more equitable society.

Whistleblowers and investigative journalism played a crucial role in uncovering the truth behind Watergate. Their bravery and commitment to the truth set a precedent for future whistleblowers, empowering them to come forward and expose corruption and wrongdoing. The role of investigative journalism in holding those in power accountable cannot be understated.

The scandal also had significant effects on international relations and diplomacy. The Watergate Scandal tarnished the reputation of the United States on the global stage, raising questions about its commitment to democracy and the rule of law. It strained relationships with other nations and undermined trust in American leadership.

Furthermore, the Watergate Scandal exposed the implications for money laundering and corruption. It revealed the potential for illicit financial activities and raised awareness about the need for stronger measures to combat money laundering and corruption at a global level.

In conclusion, the Watergate Scandal and Richard Nixon's resignation had a profound impact on global financial regulations, offshore tax havens, political fallout and resignations, legal actions and prosecutions, reforms in corporate transparency and accountability, social and economic inequality, whistleblowers and investigative journalism, international relations and diplomacy, public perception of wealth and privilege, and implications for money laundering and corruption. Its legacy serves as a constant reminder of the importance of upholding integrity and transparency in financial systems and the need for robust oversight to prevent abuses of power.

Panama Papers: Resignations of Political Figures

The Panama Papers leak in 2016 sent shockwaves across the globe, exposing a vast network of offshore tax havens and revealing the extent of global financial corruption. One of the most significant consequences of this scandal was the resignation of numerous political figures implicated in the documents. This subchapter delves into the impact of these resignations, examining the wider implications for global financial regulations, offshore tax havens, and the political fallout that ensued.

The resignations of political figures named in the Panama Papers were a clear indication of the depth of the scandal. These individuals, who held positions of power and influence, were forced to step down due to their involvement in illicit activities, such as tax evasion and money laundering. This led to a significant shift in public perception of wealth and privilege, as it became evident that even those in the highest echelons of society were not immune to scrutiny.

The resignations also triggered a series of legal actions and prosecutions. Governments worldwide were compelled to investigate and hold those accountable for their actions. This resulted in a wave of reforms in corporate transparency and accountability, as regulators sought to prevent similar scandals from occurring in the future. The Panama Papers acted as a catalyst for change in global financial regulations, prompting stricter measures to combat money laundering and corruption.

Moreover, the revelations in the Panama Papers exposed the social and economic inequality that had long been hidden behind the veil of offshore tax havens. The scandal highlighted the stark contrast between the wealthy elite and the average citizen, fueling public outrage and demands for justice. This, in turn, increased pressure on regulators to take decisive action and restore public trust in financial institutions.

The role of whistleblowers and investigative journalism cannot be overstated in the aftermath of the Panama Papers. The brave individuals who risked their livelihoods to expose the truth played a crucial role in holding the powerful accountable. Their actions shed light on the extent of corruption and sparked a global conversation about the need for transparency and integrity in politics and finance.

Furthermore, the resignations of political figures implicated in the Panama Papers had far-reaching effects on international relations and diplomacy. Countries that were directly affected by the scandal faced diplomatic challenges as the credibility of their leaders came into question. This strained relationships between nations and led to a reevaluation of existing diplomatic protocols.

In conclusion, the resignations of political figures named in the Panama Papers had a profound impact on global financial regulations, offshore tax havens, and the broader political landscape. The scandal exposed the need for reforms in corporate transparency and accountability while revealing the extent of social and economic inequality. It also emphasized the crucial role of whistleblowers and investigative journalism in uncovering corruption. The fallout from the Panama Papers continues to shape public perception of wealth and privilege, and the implications for money laundering and corruption are still being felt today. Bank regulators must remain vigilant and proactive in implementing measures to prevent such scandals from occurring in the future.

Analyzing the Impact of Political Fallout on Governance and Democracy

The political fallout resulting from financial scandals has far-reaching implications for governance and democracy. In this subchapter, we will delve into the multifaceted effects of such fallout, addressing the concerns of bank regulators and exploring various related niches.

One of the primary areas affected by political fallout is the impact on global financial regulations. Financial scandals often expose weaknesses in regulatory frameworks, prompting regulators to revisit existing policies and propose new measures to prevent similar incidents in the future. Bank regulators must closely analyze the fallout to identify gaps in oversight and develop more robust systems that can withstand the challenges posed by unethical practices.

A consequence closely linked to financial scandals is the exposure of offshore tax havens. These scandals frequently reveal the extent to which individuals and corporations exploit these havens to evade taxes, resulting in significant revenue losses for governments. As bank regulators, understanding the consequences for offshore tax havens is crucial in developing strategies to combat tax evasion and ensure a level playing field for all participants in the global financial system.

Political fallout often leads to high-profile resignations within government and corporate entities. By examining the reasons behind these resignations, bank regulators can gain valuable insights into the systemic issues that contributed to the scandal. This knowledge can inform regulatory reforms and help restore public trust in governance systems.

Legal actions and prosecutions are another aspect of political fallout. Regulators must closely monitor the legal proceedings resulting from financial scandals to understand the consequences for those involved and assess the effectiveness of existing legal frameworks. This analysis can guide regulators in strengthening legal measures against financial malpractice.

Reforms in corporate transparency and accountability are often precipitated by political fallout. As bank regulators, understanding the need for enhanced transparency and accountability measures is crucial to ensure that financial institutions operate with integrity and adhere to ethical standards.

The fallout from financial scandals often exposes social and economic inequalities that exist within societies. Bank regulators must recognize the significance of these revelations in understanding and addressing systemic issues that perpetuate inequality.

The role of whistleblowers and investigative journalism in uncovering financial scandals cannot be overstated. Bank regulators should acknowledge the importance of protecting and incentivizing whistleblowers while also supporting investigative journalists in their efforts to expose corruption and malpractice.

The effects of political fallout extend beyond national borders, impacting international relations and diplomacy. Bank regulators must consider the implications of financial scandals on the reputation and credibility of countries involved, as well as the potential consequences for global financial stability.

The public perception of wealth and privilege is often shaped by financial scandals. Bank regulators should be mindful of the public's reaction to such scandals, as it can influence public opinion on the efficacy of governance systems and their trust in financial institutions.

Lastly, political fallout sheds light on the implications for money laundering and corruption. Bank regulators must analyze the fallout to identify vulnerabilities that can be exploited for illicit activities, enabling them to strengthen anti-money laundering measures and combat corruption effectively.

In conclusion, the impact of political fallout on governance and democracy is profound and multifaceted. As bank regulators, it is essential to analyze and understand this fallout to develop effective measures that can prevent future financial scandals and promote a more transparent and accountable global financial system.

Chapter 4: Legal Actions and Prosecutions

Legal Frameworks for Addressing Financial Scandals

Financial scandals have the potential to wreak havoc on economies, undermine public trust, and disrupt global financial systems. In order to address and prevent such scandals, robust legal frameworks are crucial. This subchapter delves into the legal mechanisms that have been put in place to tackle financial scandals, with a focus on their impact on global financial regulations, consequences for offshore tax havens, political fallout and resignations, legal actions and prosecutions, reforms in corporate transparency and accountability, social and economic inequality exposed, the role of whistleblowers and investigative journalism, effects on international relations and diplomacy, public perception of wealth and privilege, and implications for money laundering and corruption.

One of the key aspects of addressing financial scandals is the strengthening of global financial regulations. International organizations such as the Financial Stability Board and the International Monetary Fund have played a significant role in developing standards and guidelines for financial institutions to prevent fraudulent activities. These regulations aim to enhance transparency, accountability, and risk management within the financial sector, thereby reducing the likelihood of scandals.

Financial scandals often involve the use of offshore tax havens to hide illicit funds and evade taxes. In response, governments and regulatory bodies have introduced stricter regulations and increased international cooperation to combat tax evasion. The implementation of initiatives such as the Common Reporting Standard and the Automatic Exchange of Information has increased transparency and made it more difficult for individuals and corporations to hide their wealth offshore.

The political fallout resulting from financial scandals is another critical area to address. Such scandals often lead to resignations of high-ranking officials, including politicians and corporate executives. In some cases, legal actions and prosecutions may be initiated against those involved. These legal actions serve as a deterrent and send a message that no one is above the law, regardless of their status or wealth.

Reforms in corporate transparency and accountability have also gained momentum in the wake of financial scandals. Governments and regulatory bodies have introduced measures to enhance the disclosure of financial information, strengthen corporate governance, and enforce ethical conduct. These reforms aim to prevent future scandals by promoting greater transparency and holding corporations accountable for their actions.

Financial scandals often expose the deep-seated social and economic inequalities within societies. They highlight the disparities between the wealthy and the less privileged, leading to public outcry and demands for change. This has prompted discussions and debates about income inequality, wealth distribution, and the need for fairer economic systems.

Whistleblowers and investigative journalism play a crucial role in uncovering financial scandals. Their efforts shed light on corrupt practices, prompting investigations and legal actions. Governments and regulatory bodies have recognized the importance of protecting whistleblowers and providing avenues for reporting wrongdoing without fear of retaliation.

Financial scandals can have far-reaching implications for international relations and diplomacy. They can strain relationships between countries and impact diplomatic efforts. The exposure of corrupt practices and money laundering can damage the reputation and credibility of nations involved, leading to strained relationships and reduced trust.

Public perception of wealth and privilege is often influenced by financial scandals. They can highlight the excesses and unethical behavior of the wealthy elite, leading to increased scrutiny and calls for wealth redistribution. Such scandals can reshape public opinion and influence attitudes towards wealth and privilege.

Lastly, financial scandals expose the vulnerabilities of systems to money laundering and corruption. They serve as a wake-up call for governments and regulatory bodies to strengthen their anti-money laundering measures and combat corruption more effectively.

In conclusion, addressing financial scandals requires a comprehensive and robust legal framework. This subchapter has explored the impact of such frameworks on global financial regulations, offshore tax havens, political fallout and resignations, legal actions and prosecutions, corporate transparency and accountability, social and economic inequality, whistleblowers and investigative journalism, international relations and diplomacy, public perception of wealth and privilege, and implications for money laundering and corruption. By implementing and enforcing these legal frameworks, bank regulators can contribute to a more transparent and accountable financial system, restoring public trust and stability.

Prosecutions and Criminal Liability

In the wake of financial scandals that have rocked the global financial industry, the issue of prosecutions and criminal liability has become a central focus. Bank regulators, in particular, are keenly interested in understanding the legal actions taken against individuals and institutions involved in these scandals. This subchapter delves into the various aspects related to prosecutions and criminal liability, shedding light on their impact on global financial regulations and the consequences for offshore tax havens.

The exposure of financial scandals has led to a surge in legal actions and prosecutions against those responsible for fraudulent activities. The fallout from these scandals has been significant, leading to political resignations and a shakeup in the financial industry. Bank regulators need to understand the repercussions of these legal actions to ensure the stability and integrity of the global financial system.

One of the major consequences of these scandals has been the tightening of global financial regulations. Governments and international organizations have recognized the need for stricter oversight and transparency to prevent similar incidents in the future. The subchapter analyzes the reforms implemented to enhance corporate transparency and accountability, which includes measures aimed at curbing money laundering and corruption.

The scandals have also exposed the social and economic inequality inherent in the financial industry. The public perception of wealth and privilege has been severely impacted, leading to a loss of trust in the system. This subchapter explores the implications of these scandals on public perception and the measures taken to address the resulting social and economic inequality.

Whistleblowers and investigative journalism have played a crucial role in uncovering these scandals. Their actions have been instrumental in bringing to light the illegal activities and holding the culprits accountable. The subchapter acknowledges the importance of these individuals and their role in exposing corruption and wrongdoing.

Furthermore, the effects of these scandals on international relations and diplomacy cannot be ignored. The subchapter examines how these incidents have strained diplomatic relations and influenced international cooperation in combating financial crimes.

Lastly, the subchapter highlights the implications for money laundering and corruption. The uncovering of these scandals has brought attention to the need for stronger measures to combat illicit financial activities and protect the integrity of the global financial system.

In summary, this subchapter on prosecutions and criminal liability provides bank regulators with a comprehensive understanding of the legal actions taken in response to financial scandals. It explores the impact on global financial regulations, consequences for offshore tax havens, political fallout and resignations, reforms in corporate transparency and accountability, social and economic inequality exposed, the role of whistleblowers and investigative journalism, effects on international relations and diplomacy, public perception of wealth and privilege, and the implications for money laundering and corruption. This knowledge is crucial for regulators to address the challenges posed by financial scandals and ensure the stability and integrity of the global financial system.

Civil Litigation and Financial Compensation

In the wake of financial scandals that have rocked the global economy, civil litigation and financial compensation have become significant components in holding individuals and corporations accountable for their actions. This subchapter explores the implications of civil litigation and the pursuit of financial compensation in the aftermath of these scandals.

One of the most crucial aspects impacted by civil litigation is global financial regulations. As bank regulators, it is essential to understand how these scandals have influenced regulatory frameworks worldwide. The exposure of fraudulent activities and the subsequent legal actions have prompted regulators to reassess existing regulations and introduce new measures to prevent similar occurrences in the future.

Additionally, the consequences for offshore tax havens cannot be ignored. These scandals have shed light on the role played by these havens in facilitating illicit financial activities. As a result, bank regulators are now more determined to crack down on tax evasion and money laundering, leading to stricter regulations and increased international cooperation in combating these issues.

The political fallout and resignations that often follow financial scandals have far-reaching implications. This subchapter delves into the impact on public trust in institutions and the subsequent calls for accountability and transparency. The legal actions and prosecutions initiated against those involved in the scandals serve as a warning to individuals and corporations that such behavior will not be tolerated.

Reforms in corporate transparency and accountability are a direct outcome of these scandals. Bank regulators must stay abreast of the latest developments in this area, as efforts to enhance transparency and accountability will require their active participation. The subchapter explores the potential reforms and their impact on financial institutions and their clients.

Furthermore, the scandals have exposed the stark social and economic inequality that exists within societies. This subchapter discusses the wider implications of this inequality and its potential to undermine social stability. It also delves into the role of whistleblowers and investigative journalism in uncovering these scandals and the importance of protecting those who expose corruption.

The effects on international relations and diplomacy cannot be underestimated. As bank regulators, understanding how these scandals impact diplomatic relations and cooperation between countries is crucial. It provides insights into the potential challenges and opportunities that arise from these incidents.

The public perception of wealth and privilege has also been significantly affected. This subchapter explores how these scandals have shaped public opinion and how their perception of the wealthy and privileged has changed. It also examines how these changes may influence public sentiment towards financial institutions and regulators.

Finally, the implications for money laundering and corruption are examined in detail. The scandals have exposed vulnerabilities in the existing systems, necessitating a reevaluation of anti-money laundering measures and efforts to combat corruption.

In conclusion, civil litigation and financial compensation play a vital role in the aftermath of financial scandals. As bank regulators, it is essential to understand the wide-ranging implications of these legal actions and their impact on global financial regulations, offshore tax havens, political fallout, legal actions and prosecutions, corporate transparency and accountability, social and economic inequality, whistleblowers, investigative journalism, international relations and diplomacy, public perception of wealth and privilege, and the fight against money laundering and corruption. By comprehending these implications, bank regulators can contribute to shaping a more transparent and accountable financial system.

Challenges in Prosecuting Financial Crimes

Financial crimes, such as fraud, money laundering, and corruption, have long plagued the global financial system, causing significant damage to economies, institutions, and individuals. However, prosecuting these crimes presents numerous challenges that hinder the effective enforcement of financial regulations and the pursuit of justice. This subchapter delves into the key challenges faced by regulators and law enforcement agencies when it comes to prosecuting financial crimes.

One of the primary challenges is the complex nature of financial crimes. Perpetrators often employ sophisticated techniques to conceal their illicit activities, making it difficult for investigators to gather evidence and build a strong case. These crimes often involve intricate money trails, offshore accounts, and complex financial transactions that require specialized knowledge and expertise to unravel.

Moreover, financial crimes frequently transcend national borders, posing jurisdictional challenges. Offshore tax havens and secretive jurisdictions make it easier for criminals to hide their assets and evade legal consequences. Coordinating investigations and prosecutions across different jurisdictions is a complex and time-consuming process, often requiring international cooperation and mutual legal assistance treaties.

Another hurdle lies in the political fallout and potential consequences for offshore tax havens. High-profile financial scandals can expose the role of these tax havens in facilitating illicit financial flows, damaging their reputation and credibility. As a result, political pressure to protect offshore financial centers may hinder effective prosecution and deter meaningful reforms.

Additionally, prosecuting financial crimes involving powerful individuals or corporations can be met with resistance and intimidation. Political influence, deep pockets, and access to top-notch legal representation can create an uneven playing field, making it difficult to secure convictions. The fear of damaging international relations or causing economic instability may further impede efforts to bring those responsible to justice.

Furthermore, the public perception of wealth and privilege can influence the outcome of prosecutions. In societies where the gap between the rich and the poor is wide, there may be a perception that the wealthy can buy their way out of legal troubles. This can erode public trust in the justice system and undermine the legitimacy of prosecutions.

Despite these challenges, there have been notable successes in prosecuting financial crimes. Whistleblowers and investigative journalism have played a crucial role in uncovering wrongdoing and providing invaluable evidence. Reforms in corporate transparency and accountability, as well as increased international cooperation, have also contributed to more effective prosecutions.

In conclusion, prosecuting financial crimes is a complex and multifaceted endeavor. Overcoming challenges related to the complexity of these crimes, jurisdictional issues, political pressure, and public perception is essential for enforcing financial regulations and holding perpetrators accountable. Only through concerted efforts, collaboration, and meaningful reforms can we hope to combat financial crimes effectively and safeguard the integrity of the global financial system.

Case Studies: Landmark Legal Actions and Prosecutions

Title: Case Studies: Landmark Legal Actions and Prosecutions

Introduction:

The subchapter "Case Studies: Landmark Legal Actions and Prosecutions" delves into the various high-profile legal actions and prosecutions that have occurred as a result of financial scandals. This section aims to provide bank regulators with in-depth insights into the consequences, implications, and reforms that have emerged from these cases. By examining specific examples from different regions and industries, this subchapter sheds light on the transformative effects of these legal actions and their impact on global financial regulations, offshore tax havens, political fallout, and more.

1. Historical Context and Global Impact:

This section begins by providing a historical overview of some landmark legal actions and prosecutions, emphasizing their global impact on financial regulations. It delves into cases such as the Enron scandal, the Bernie Madoff Ponzi scheme, and the Panama Papers leak, highlighting the catalytic role of these cases in shaping international financial standards.

2. Consequences for Offshore Tax Havens:

This part focuses on the consequences of legal actions and prosecutions on offshore tax havens. It explores how these cases have exposed the illicit activities taking place in these jurisdictions, leading to international pressure for transparency and tighter regulations. It examines prominent cases such as the LuxLeaks and SwissLeaks scandals, which have resulted in significant changes in how offshore tax havens operate.

3. Political Fallout and Resignations:

This section delves into the political fallout and high-profile resignations that have occurred as a result of legal actions and prosecutions. It provides case studies of politicians, government officials, and corporate executives who faced legal consequences, highlighting the public outcry and loss of public trust in these individuals and their institutions.

4. Reforms in Corporate Transparency and Accountability:

This part examines the reforms that emerged from these legal actions, focusing on the enhancement of corporate transparency and accountability. It discusses the implementation of stricter regulations, such as the Foreign Corrupt Practices Act (FCPA) and the Dodd-Frank Act, as well as the establishment of international bodies like the Financial Action Task Force (FATF) to combat money laundering and corruption.

5. Role of Whistleblowers and Investigative Journalism:

This section explores the crucial role played by whistleblowers and investigative journalism in uncovering financial scandals and initiating legal actions. It examines cases such as Edward Snowden's revelations and the work of journalists at organizations like WikiLeaks, emphasizing their impact on public perception and the demand for increased accountability.

6. Effects on International Relations and Diplomacy:

This part analyzes the effects of legal actions on international relations and diplomacy. It discusses the strain caused by the exposure of illicit financial activities involving foreign entities, leading to diplomatic tensions and the imposition of sanctions. It also explores efforts to foster international cooperation and collaboration in combating financial crimes.

7. Public Perception of Wealth and Privilege:

This section delves into how legal actions and prosecutions have shaped public perception regarding wealth and privilege. It examines the widening wealth gap and the public's growing awareness of the unequal distribution of wealth, leading to demands for reforms and increased social and economic equality.

8. Implications for Money Laundering and Corruption:

This final part discusses the implications of legal actions on money laundering and corruption. It explores the evolving methods used by criminals and the measures taken to counter these illicit activities, including the adoption of digital technologies and AI-driven solutions in detecting and preventing financial crimes.

Conclusion:

The case studies presented in this subchapter highlight the far-reaching impact of legal actions and prosecutions on various aspects of the global financial landscape. By examining these landmark cases, bank regulators gain valuable insights into the consequences, reforms, and implications that emerge from such events. The comprehensive understanding gained from these examples can guide regulators in their efforts to strengthen financial regulations, combat money laundering, enhance transparency, and foster greater accountability in the banking sector.

Chapter 5: Reforms in Corporate Transparency and Accountability

Importance of Corporate Transparency and Accountability

In recent years, financial scandals have rocked the global economy, resulting in significant political fallout, resignations, and legal actions. These events have shed light on the critical importance of corporate transparency and accountability in maintaining the stability and integrity of the financial system. This subchapter explores the far-reaching implications of these scandals, specifically focusing on the impact on global financial regulations, consequences for offshore tax havens, political fallout and resignations, legal actions and prosecutions, reforms in corporate transparency and accountability, social and economic inequality exposed, the role of whistleblowers and investigative journalism, effects on international relations and diplomacy, public perception of wealth and privilege, and implications for money laundering and corruption.

The financial scandals that have unfolded in recent years have highlighted the urgent need for enhanced global financial regulations. Bank regulators play a crucial role in ensuring that financial institutions comply with these regulations and maintain transparency in their operations. The scandals have exposed weaknesses in the regulatory framework, prompting regulators to re-evaluate their oversight mechanisms and implement stricter regulations to prevent future misconduct.

Offshore tax havens have long been a concern for regulators, as they facilitate tax evasion and money laundering. The scandals have brought increased scrutiny to these jurisdictions, resulting in international pressure to crack down on tax havens and enforce stricter regulations. Regulators must work collaboratively to address these issues and close the loopholes that allow corporations and individuals to evade taxes and hide illicit funds.

The political fallout and resignations resulting from these scandals have created a crisis of public confidence in the financial industry. The misconduct and unethical behavior of corporate executives have eroded trust in financial institutions, necessitating swift action to hold individuals accountable and restore public trust. Regulators must ensure that those responsible for the wrongdoing face legal consequences and are held personally liable for their actions.

Reforms in corporate transparency and accountability are crucial to preventing future financial scandals. Regulators must push for greater transparency in corporate governance, ensuring that companies disclose accurate and timely information to investors and the public. Additionally, regulators should encourage the adoption of robust internal controls and risk management practices to prevent misconduct and unethical behavior.

The financial scandals have exposed the stark reality of social and economic inequality. The revelations of excessive executive compensation, tax avoidance, and fraudulent practices have intensified public scrutiny of wealth and privilege. Regulators must address these issues by advocating for fairer wealth distribution and implementing policies that promote economic equality.

Whistleblowers and investigative journalism have played a pivotal role in exposing financial misconduct. Regulators should encourage and protect whistleblowers, as they provide valuable information that can help uncover wrongdoing and hold those responsible accountable. Additionally, regulators should collaborate with investigative journalists to expose financial irregularities and promote transparency in the financial sector.

The scandals have also had significant implications for international relations and diplomacy. Governments worldwide must work together to combat money laundering and corruption, as these issues transcend national borders. Regulators should strengthen international cooperation and information sharing to effectively combat these illicit activities.

Public perception of wealth and privilege has been profoundly affected by these scandals. The excessive wealth and extravagant lifestyles of corporate executives have fueled public anger and resentment. Regulators must address this issue by promoting greater transparency in executive compensation and corporate governance, ensuring that companies are held accountable for their actions.

Lastly, the scandals have exposed the prevalence of money laundering and corruption within the financial system. Regulators must take decisive action to strengthen anti-money laundering measures, impose stricter regulations, and collaborate with law enforcement agencies to combat these illicit activities effectively.

In conclusion, corporate transparency and accountability are of paramount importance in maintaining the stability and integrity of the global financial system. Regulators play a crucial role in enforcing regulations, holding individuals accountable, and promoting reforms that prevent future scandals. By addressing the impact on global financial regulations, consequences for offshore tax havens, political fallout and resignations, legal actions and prosecutions, reforms in corporate transparency and accountability, social and economic inequality, the role of whistleblowers and investigative journalism, effects on international relations and diplomacy, public perception of wealth and privilege, and implications for money laundering and corruption, regulators can work towards restoring public trust and ensuring a more transparent and accountable financial industry.

Corporate Governance Reforms

The deep dive into financial scandals has revealed a pressing need for corporate governance reforms. These scandals have exposed the vulnerabilities within the global financial system, resulting in severe consequences for both the regulators and the offshore tax havens. The political fallout and subsequent resignations have further highlighted the urgent need for changes in corporate transparency and accountability.

One of the key aspects of corporate governance reforms is the establishment of stricter regulations to ensure the integrity of the financial sector. This includes measures to prevent money laundering and corruption, two issues that have been exacerbated by the scandals. By implementing more rigorous checks and balances, bank regulators can restore public trust and confidence in the financial system.

Moreover, these reforms also aim to address the social and economic inequality that has been brought to light. The scandals have exposed the vast disparities in wealth and privilege, leading to public outrage. By holding corporations accountable for their actions and ensuring fair distribution of resources, these reforms can help address the underlying issues of inequality and promote a more inclusive society.

Whistleblowers and investigative journalism have played a crucial role in uncovering these scandals. Therefore, it is essential to protect and encourage the role of whistleblowers in exposing corporate wrongdoing. Additionally, investigative journalism should be supported and given the necessary resources to continue their important work in uncovering financial misconduct.

The impact of these scandals extends beyond national borders, affecting international relations and diplomacy. Rebuilding trust and cooperation between countries becomes imperative to prevent future financial crises. Collaborative efforts in sharing information and implementing global financial regulations are crucial to prevent offshore tax havens from becoming safe havens for illicit activities.

The legal actions and prosecutions resulting from these scandals serve as a deterrent for future corporate misconduct. Holding individuals and corporations accountable for their actions sends a strong message that unethical practices will not be tolerated. These legal proceedings also help in restoring public confidence in the justice system.

Furthermore, the public perception of wealth and privilege has been significantly impacted by these scandals. The exposure of the corrupt practices of the ultra-rich has led to a reevaluation of societal values and norms. Society now demands greater transparency and fairness from corporations, leading to a shift in public opinion on the distribution of wealth.

Finally, the implications for money laundering and corruption cannot be ignored. Stricter regulations and increased transparency are vital in preventing these illegal activities from thriving. By implementing effective measures, bank regulators can ensure that the financial system is not misused for illicit purposes, ultimately safeguarding the global economy.

In conclusion, the financial scandals have necessitated comprehensive corporate governance reforms. These reforms encompass various aspects, including global financial regulations, offshore tax havens, political fallout and resignations, legal actions and prosecutions, corporate transparency and accountability, social and economic inequality, whistleblowers and investigative journalism, international relations and diplomacy, public perception of wealth and privilege, and implications for money laundering and corruption. By addressing these issues, bank regulators can promote a more transparent and resilient financial system that is accountable to both the public and the global community.

Enhancing Board Independence and Oversight

In the wake of numerous financial scandals that have shaken the global financial landscape, it has become imperative for bank regulators to address the issue of enhancing board independence and oversight. The repercussions of these scandals have had far-reaching effects on various aspects of the financial industry, including global financial regulations, offshore tax havens, political fallout and resignations, legal actions and prosecutions, reforms in corporate transparency and accountability, social and economic inequality, the role of whistleblowers and investigative journalism, effects on international relations and diplomacy, public perception of wealth and privilege, and implications for money laundering and corruption.

The need to strengthen board independence and oversight arises from the realization that many of these financial scandals were facilitated by the lack of effective oversight and the presence of conflicts of interest within corporate boards. In several cases, board members were found to have personal connections or financial interests that compromised their ability to act in the best interests of the company and its stakeholders. This has led to a loss of public trust in the integrity of the financial system and the need for regulatory intervention.

To address this issue, bank regulators must introduce and enforce stringent guidelines that promote board independence and minimize conflicts of interest. This could include measures such as ensuring a majority of independent directors on corporate boards, establishing robust risk management and internal control systems, implementing regular board evaluations, and enhancing transparency in board decision-making processes.

Additionally, regulators should encourage the appointment of directors with diverse backgrounds and expertise to ensure a more holistic and comprehensive oversight of financial institutions. This can help prevent groupthink and promote a culture of accountability and transparency.

Furthermore, regulators must also enhance their own oversight and monitoring mechanisms to ensure that financial institutions adhere to the prescribed guidelines. This may involve conducting regular audits, inspections, and investigations, as well as imposing severe penalties for non-compliance.

By enhancing board independence and oversight, bank regulators can not only restore public trust in the financial system but also mitigate the risk of future financial scandals. This will have a positive impact on global financial regulations, offshore tax havens, political stability, legal actions and prosecutions, corporate transparency and accountability, social and economic inequality, the role of whistleblowers and investigative journalism, international relations and diplomacy, public perception of wealth and privilege, and the fight against money laundering and corruption.

In conclusion, enhancing board independence and oversight is crucial in the aftermath of financial scandals. By implementing stricter guidelines and promoting transparency and accountability, bank regulators can play a vital role in preventing future financial misconduct and rebuilding public trust in the global financial system.

Strengthening Executive Compensation Practices

In the wake of numerous financial scandals that have rocked the global economy, it has become increasingly clear that executive compensation practices play a significant role in incentivizing unethical behavior and exacerbating the risks associated with offshore tax havens, money laundering, and corruption. This subchapter explores the need for strengthened executive compensation practices to address the impact on global financial regulations, consequences for offshore tax havens, political fallout and resignations, legal actions and prosecutions, reforms in corporate transparency and accountability, social and economic inequality exposed, the role of whistleblowers and investigative journalism, effects on international relations and diplomacy, public perception of wealth and privilege, and implications for money laundering and corruption.

To effectively address these issues, bank regulators must prioritize the alignment of executive compensation with long-term sustainable performance and risk management. This can be achieved by implementing several key reforms. Firstly, the use of stock options and bonuses tied to short-term financial performance should be reduced in favor of long-term performance metrics, such as sustainable growth, customer satisfaction, and ethical conduct.

Furthermore, transparency and accountability in executive compensation should be enhanced. Regulators should require companies to disclose detailed information about the structure and rationale behind executive pay packages, including the use of performance benchmarks and the alignment of incentives with societal and environmental goals.

In addition, clawback provisions should be strengthened to allow companies to recover executive compensation in cases of misconduct or fraudulent behavior. This would serve as a powerful deterrent against unethical practices and signal the commitment of regulators to hold executives accountable for their actions.

Moreover, regulators should encourage the establishment of independent compensation committees composed of individuals with diverse backgrounds and expertise. These committees should be responsible for setting executive pay, ensuring that it is aligned with the long-term interests of the company and its stakeholders.

By implementing these reforms, bank regulators can contribute to a more equitable and sustainable financial system. Strengthening executive compensation practices will not only reduce the incentives for unethical behavior but also restore public trust in the banking sector. Ultimately, it is crucial for regulators to work collaboratively with financial institutions to ensure that executive compensation aligns with the values of transparency, accountability, and long-term sustainability. Only then can we hope to prevent future financial scandals and promote a more stable and fair global economy.

Regulatory Frameworks for Corporate Transparency

In the wake of numerous financial scandals that have rocked the global economy, it has become increasingly clear that strong regulatory frameworks for corporate transparency are crucial to prevent such occurrences in the future. This subchapter delves into the various aspects of regulatory frameworks that are essential in maintaining integrity, accountability, and transparency within the corporate sector.

The impact of financial scandals on global financial regulations cannot be underestimated. These scandals have highlighted the need for stricter oversight and more robust regulations to prevent corporate malpractice and ensure the stability of the global financial system. Bank regulators play a pivotal role in creating and implementing these regulations, ensuring that they are adhered to, and taking necessary actions against those who violate them.

One consequence of financial scandals that cannot be ignored is their impact on offshore tax havens. Such scandals have exposed the vulnerabilities of these havens, which have long been accused of facilitating tax evasion and money laundering. Consequently, regulators are now under pressure to tighten regulations and close loopholes that allow individuals and corporations to hide their assets offshore.

The political fallout and resignations that often accompany financial scandals have far-reaching implications. They erode public trust in the financial sector and raise questions about the integrity of those in power. To restore public confidence, regulators must ensure thorough investigations are conducted, and legal actions and prosecutions are pursued against those responsible.

Reforms in corporate transparency and accountability are necessary to prevent future financial scandals. Regulators should focus on enhancing disclosure requirements, strengthening internal controls, and promoting responsible corporate governance practices. These reforms should also address the social and economic inequality that is often exposed by financial scandals, aiming to create a more equitable and just society.

Whistleblowers and investigative journalism have played a crucial role in exposing financial scandals. Regulators must recognize and protect the rights of whistleblowers, incentivizing them to come forward with information that can help identify and prevent corporate misconduct. Collaborating with investigative journalists can also aid in uncovering hidden truths and holding wrongdoers accountable.

The effects of financial scandals on international relations and diplomacy cannot be ignored. Such scandals often involve cross-border transactions and illicit activities, straining relationships between countries. Regulators must work together to harmonize regulations, share information, and cooperate in combating money laundering and corruption.

Public perception of wealth and privilege is deeply impacted by financial scandals. The exposure of illicit activities and corrupt practices can lead to a loss of public trust in the wealthy and powerful. Regulators must address this by enforcing regulations that promote transparency and fairness, ensuring that the public perceives wealth as earned through legitimate means.

Finally, financial scandals have significant implications for money laundering and corruption. Regulators must strengthen anti-money laundering measures, enhance due diligence requirements, and encourage the reporting of suspicious transactions. By doing so, they can contribute to a more transparent and accountable global financial system.

In conclusion, regulatory frameworks for corporate transparency are crucial in preventing financial scandals and maintaining the integrity of the global financial system. Bank regulators play a vital role in creating and enforcing these frameworks, which have far-reaching implications for global financial regulations, offshore tax havens, political fallout and resignations, legal actions and prosecutions, corporate transparency and accountability, social and economic inequality, whistleblowers and investigative journalism, international relations and diplomacy, public perception of wealth and privilege, as well as money laundering and corruption. By implementing robust regulations and promoting transparency, regulators can protect the interests of the public and ensure a fair and stable financial environment.

Sarbanes-Oxley Act

The Sarbanes-Oxley Act (SOX) is a landmark piece of legislation passed in response to the accounting scandals that rocked the corporate world in the early 2000s. Named after its sponsors, Senator Paul Sarbanes and Representative Michael Oxley, the act aimed to restore public trust in financial reporting and corporate governance.

Impact on Global Financial Regulations:

The passage of the Sarbanes-Oxley Act had far-reaching implications for global financial regulations. Many countries adopted similar measures to strengthen their own corporate governance practices and enhance transparency in financial reporting. The act served as a catalyst for international efforts to combat fraud and protect investors.

Consequences for Offshore Tax Havens:

SOX also had significant consequences for offshore tax havens. These havens, known for their lax regulations and secrecy, became less attractive to companies looking to evade taxes or engage in fraudulent activities. The act imposed stricter reporting requirements and increased scrutiny on offshore financial transactions, resulting in a decline in offshore tax evasion and money laundering.

Political Fallout and Resignations:

The financial scandals that prompted the Sarbanes-Oxley Act led to a wave of political fallout and high-profile resignations. Corporate executives and auditors faced criminal charges, and several major companies collapsed as a result of their fraudulent activities. The act aimed to hold these individuals accountable and restore public confidence in the financial system.

Legal Actions and Prosecutions:

SOX empowered regulatory bodies, such as the Securities and Exchange Commission (SEC), to enforce stricter regulations and impose harsher penalties on corporate wrongdoers. The act introduced criminal penalties for securities fraud and obstruction of justice, leading to increased prosecutions and legal actions against individuals involved in financial misconduct.

Reforms in Corporate Transparency and Accountability:

One of the key objectives of the Sarbanes-Oxley Act was to enhance corporate transparency and accountability. The act established stringent reporting requirements, including the certification of financial statements by CEOs and CFOs. It also mandated the establishment of independent audit committees and the prohibition of certain non-audit services by external auditors.

Social and Economic Inequality Exposed:

The financial scandals that preceded the passage of SOX laid bare the social and economic inequalities within corporate America. The act aimed to address these disparities by promoting fairness, accountability, and transparency in corporate governance. It sought to protect the interests of shareholders and employees, ensuring that executives were held accountable for their actions.

Role of Whistleblowers and Investigative Journalism:

SOX encouraged the role of whistleblowers in exposing corporate fraud and misconduct. The act provided protection for individuals who reported such activities and offered financial incentives for their cooperation. Additionally, investigative journalism played a crucial role in uncovering and publicizing financial scandals, leading to greater public awareness and pressure for regulatory reform.

Effects on International Relations and Diplomacy:

The passage of the Sarbanes-Oxley Act had implications for international relations and diplomacy. It affected cross-border investments and trade by imposing stricter regulations on foreign companies listed on U.S. stock exchanges. It also led to increased cooperation between regulatory bodies of different countries in combating financial fraud and promoting global financial stability.

Public Perception of Wealth and Privilege:

The financial scandals and subsequent passage of SOX had a profound impact on public perception of wealth and privilege. The act exposed the dark underbelly of corporate America, highlighting the unethical practices of powerful executives. It led to a widespread public backlash against corporate greed and a demand for greater accountability and fairness.

Implications for Money Laundering and Corruption:

SOX had significant implications for the fight against money laundering and corruption. By strengthening financial reporting requirements and increasing scrutiny on financial transactions, the act made it harder for individuals and companies to engage in illicit activities. It marked a significant step towards deterring money laundering and promoting transparency in global financial transactions.

The Sarbanes-Oxley Act represents a turning point in financial regulation and corporate governance. Its impact on global financial regulations, consequences for offshore tax havens, political fallout and resignations, legal actions and prosecutions, reforms in corporate transparency and accountability, social and economic inequality, role of whistleblowers and investigative journalism, effects on international relations and diplomacy, public perception of wealth and privilege, and implications for money laundering and corruption cannot be overstated. The act serves as a constant reminder of the importance of ethical behavior, transparency, and accountability in the corporate world.

European Union's Transparency Directive

The European Union's Transparency Directive has had a significant impact on global financial regulations, particularly in the aftermath of several high-profile financial scandals. This subchapter will delve into the key provisions and implications of the Directive, addressing its consequences for offshore tax havens, political fallout and resignations, legal actions and prosecutions, reforms in corporate transparency and accountability, social and economic inequality, the role of whistleblowers and investigative journalism, effects on international relations and diplomacy, public perception of wealth and privilege, and implications for money laundering and corruption.

The Transparency Directive, implemented in 2004, aimed to enhance transparency and investor protection across EU member states. Its main objectives were to harmonize reporting requirements for issuers of securities and to ensure the timely disclosure of information that could impact investors' decisions. The Directive mandated that all companies whose securities are traded on regulated markets must disclose certain financial and non-financial information to the public.

One of the immediate consequences of the Directive was its impact on offshore tax havens. With increased transparency requirements, it became more difficult for individuals and corporations to hide their assets and evade taxes through offshore entities. This resulted in a crackdown on tax havens and a shift towards greater cooperation between countries in combating tax avoidance and evasion.

The Directive also had significant political fallout and led to high-profile resignations. Several politicians and government officials were implicated in financial scandals, and public trust in the political establishment eroded. As a result, there were calls for legal actions and prosecutions to hold those responsible accountable for their actions.

To address the shortcomings revealed by the scandals, the Transparency Directive prompted reforms in corporate transparency and accountability. Companies were required to disclose more detailed information about their financial performance, corporate governance practices, and environmental and social impacts. This shift towards greater transparency aimed to restore public trust in the corporate sector and prevent future financial misconduct.

The Directive also shed light on social and economic inequality, exposing the vast disparities in wealth and privilege. The public perception of the wealthy elite and the privileged few became increasingly critical, leading to demands for greater income redistribution and social justice.

Whistleblowers and investigative journalism played a crucial role in uncovering the financial scandals and bringing them to light. The Transparency Directive acknowledged the importance of whistleblowers in exposing wrongdoing and provided legal protections for those who come forward with valuable information. This recognition empowered whistleblowers and incentivized investigative journalism, leading to further revelations of corruption and malpractice.

On an international level, the Transparency Directive had implications for international relations and diplomacy. It put pressure on non-EU countries to adopt similar transparency measures to avoid being labeled as tax havens and to maintain favorable trade relations with the EU.

The public perception of wealth and privilege underwent a significant shift as a result of the Directive. The scandals exposed the extent of corruption and unethical behavior within the financial industry, leading to public outrage and a reevaluation of societal values.

Furthermore, the Directive had implications for money laundering and corruption. By increasing transparency and disclosure requirements, it became more challenging for illicit funds to be laundered through complex financial structures. This helped in the fight against money laundering and corruption, forcing criminals to find alternative methods to hide their illegal activities.

In conclusion, the European Union's Transparency Directive has had far-reaching implications for global financial regulations. It has exposed the consequences of offshore tax havens, led to political fallout and resignations, spurred legal actions and prosecutions, prompted reforms in corporate transparency and accountability, exposed social and economic inequality, empowered whistleblowers and investigative journalism, influenced international relations and diplomacy, reshaped public perception of wealth and privilege, and impacted money laundering and corruption. The Directive has played a significant role in addressing the fallout from financial scandals and has been instrumental in promoting greater transparency and accountability in the global financial system.

Evaluating the Effectiveness of Reforms in Corporate Transparency

In the wake of numerous financial scandals and the subsequent political fallout and resignations, the need for effective reforms in corporate transparency and accountability has become paramount. As bank regulators, it is essential to evaluate the effectiveness of these reforms and understand their implications on various aspects of the global financial system.

One of the key impacts of reforms in corporate transparency is their effect on global financial regulations. These reforms aim to enhance regulatory frameworks and improve oversight mechanisms, ensuring that companies adhere to ethical standards and disclose accurate financial information. By strengthening global financial regulations, these reforms help restore trust in the financial system, enhance investor confidence, and promote stability in the global economy.

Another crucial consequence of these reforms is their impact on offshore tax havens. The enhanced transparency and accountability measures make it harder for individuals and corporations to hide their wealth and evade taxes in these jurisdictions. This, in turn, reduces the attractiveness of offshore tax havens and discourages illicit financial activities, thus contributing to a fairer and more equitable global tax system.

The political fallout and resignations resulting from financial scandals often create a sense of urgency for reform. These scandals expose the flaws in the existing system, leading to public outrage and demands for stricter regulations and increased corporate accountability. The effectiveness of reforms can be evaluated by assessing their ability to address these political ramifications and prevent future scandals, thereby restoring public trust in institutions and individuals responsible for financial governance.

Reforms in corporate transparency also have significant legal implications. They often lead to increased legal actions and prosecutions against individuals and corporations involved in fraudulent activities. By holding wrongdoers accountable, these reforms act as a deterrent against future misconduct, ensuring that justice is served and restoring faith in the legal system.

Furthermore, these reforms highlight the crucial role of whistleblowers and investigative journalism in exposing financial misconduct. By providing protection and incentives for whistleblowers, reforms encourage individuals to come forward with information, helping uncover corruption and fraudulent practices. Investigative journalism plays a vital role in exposing such scandals and holding those responsible accountable.

The effects of reforms in corporate transparency extend beyond national boundaries. They have implications for international relations and diplomacy, as countries cooperate to combat money laundering and corruption. By aligning their regulatory frameworks and sharing information, countries can enhance their ability to fight financial crimes and promote integrity in the global financial system.

In conclusion, evaluating the effectiveness of reforms in corporate transparency is crucial for bank regulators. These reforms have far-reaching consequences, impacting global financial regulations, offshore tax havens, political fallout and resignations, legal actions and prosecutions, social and economic inequality, whistleblowers and investigative journalism, international relations and diplomacy, public perception of wealth and privilege, as well as implications for money laundering and corruption. By critically assessing the outcomes of these reforms, bank regulators can ensure that they effectively address the problems plaguing the financial system, restore public trust, and promote a fairer and more transparent global economy.

Chapter 6: Social and Economic Inequality Exposed

Link between Financial Scandals and Inequality

Financial scandals have long been associated with exacerbating social and economic inequality. These scandals, often involving fraudulent activities, insider trading, and corporate malfeasance, have far-reaching consequences that go beyond the immediate financial impact. In fact, they have the potential to reshape global financial regulations, impact offshore tax havens, trigger political fallout and resignations, lead to legal actions and prosecutions, necessitate reforms in corporate transparency and accountability, expose social and economic inequality, highlight the crucial role of whistleblowers and investigative journalism, affect international relations and diplomacy, shape public perception of wealth and privilege, and have implications for money laundering and corruption.

One of the most significant consequences of financial scandals is their impact on global financial regulations. These scandals often expose loopholes and weaknesses in existing regulatory frameworks, compelling bank regulators to reassess and tighten their oversight and enforcement mechanisms. The fallout from scandals such as Enron, Lehman Brothers, and the recent Panama Papers has led to increased scrutiny of offshore tax havens. Regulators are now more vigilant in identifying and cracking down on tax evasion and illicit financial flows, which ultimately contribute to reducing inequality by ensuring a fairer distribution of wealth and resources.

Furthermore, financial scandals have wide-ranging political ramifications. When high-profile individuals or corporations are implicated in fraudulent activities, public trust in the political system is eroded. Consequently, politicians and government officials may face severe backlash, leading to resignations, calls for reform, and even changes in the political landscape. These scandals also result in legal actions and prosecutions, as authorities seek to hold the perpetrators accountable for their actions. The legal consequences of financial scandals can range from hefty fines and sanctions to imprisonment, serving as a deterrent for future misconduct.

In addition to the immediate repercussions, financial scandals shed light on the urgent need for reforms in corporate transparency and accountability. The exposure of unethical practices and corporate greed prompts calls for increased transparency, stricter regulations, and enhanced corporate governance. These reforms aim to prevent future scandals, protect shareholders and investors, and promote a more equitable distribution of wealth.

Perhaps one of the most significant impacts of financial scandals is the exposure of social and economic inequality. These scandals often unveil the stark disparities between the wealthy elite and the average citizen. The revelation that a select few can engage in illicit activities to amass enormous wealth while the majority struggle to make ends meet fuels public outrage and demands for systemic change. Financial scandals become a catalyst for discussions on income inequality, wealth distribution, and social justice.

Whistleblowers and investigative journalism play a crucial role in uncovering financial scandals. Their courage and diligence in exposing corruption, fraud, and illegal activities ensure that the truth is brought to light. Without their efforts, many scandals would remain hidden, perpetuating inequality and allowing the powerful to exploit the system.

The effects of financial scandals extend beyond national borders, impacting international relations and diplomacy. Scandals involving offshore tax havens, for instance, strain diplomatic relations between countries and undermine trust in the global financial system. Cooperation and coordination among nations become imperative to combat money laundering, corruption, and illicit financial flows.

Financial scandals also influence public perception of wealth and privilege. They highlight the excesses and abuses of a select few while the majority face economic hardships. As a result, public sentiment towards the wealthy elite and the financial sector can turn hostile, further fueling demands for reform and equality.

Finally, financial scandals have profound implications for money laundering and corruption. The exposure of illicit financial activities and the subsequent crackdown on such practices disrupts the flow of illicit funds, reducing opportunities for money laundering and corruption. This, in turn, contributes to a more transparent and accountable financial system.

In conclusion, the link between financial scandals and inequality is undeniable. These scandals have far-reaching consequences that impact global financial regulations, offshore tax havens, political dynamics, legal actions, corporate transparency, social and economic inequality, whistleblowers, international relations, public perception, money laundering, and corruption. Understanding and addressing this link is essential for bank regulators aiming to create a more equitable and just financial system.

Consequences of Inequality on Society and Economy

In the aftermath of financial scandals and the subsequent political fallout and resignations, it is crucial for bank regulators to understand the far-reaching consequences of inequality on society and the economy. This subchapter delves into the various ways in which inequality impacts global financial regulations, offshore tax havens, political dynamics, legal actions, corporate transparency, social and economic inequality, whistleblowers, international relations, public perception, as well as money laundering and corruption.

One of the most significant consequences of inequality on society and the economy is its impact on global financial regulations. Wealthy individuals and corporations often exploit offshore tax havens to evade taxes and hide their assets, exacerbating the problem of income inequality. As a result, bank regulators must work towards implementing stricter regulations to prevent such practices and ensure a more equitable distribution of wealth.

The political fallout and resignations triggered by financial scandals highlight the deep-rooted corruption within the system. Legal actions and prosecutions are necessary to hold those responsible accountable and restore public trust. Bank regulators have a crucial role in ensuring that these actions are taken and that reforms are implemented to enhance corporate transparency and accountability.

Inequality not only has social implications but also economic consequences. It widens the gap between the rich and the poor, leading to social unrest and a lack of economic mobility. It hampers the overall growth of the economy and creates an unstable environment. Bank regulators need to recognize the importance of addressing inequality to foster a more sustainable and prosperous economy.

Whistleblowers and investigative journalism play a vital role in exposing financial scandals and holding those responsible accountable. Bank regulators should encourage and protect whistleblowers, as they provide crucial information that can help prevent future scandals. Additionally, international relations and diplomacy can be strained as offshore tax havens and corruption undermine trust and cooperation between nations.

The public perception of wealth and privilege also changes in the face of financial scandals. These events expose the flaws in the system and highlight the unfair advantages enjoyed by the wealthy. As a result, there is an increased demand for reforms that promote equality and fairness.

Lastly, financial scandals often reveal the extent of money laundering and corruption within the system. Bank regulators must take steps to combat these illicit activities to maintain the integrity of the financial sector and restore public trust.

In conclusion, the consequences of inequality on society and the economy are vast and far-reaching. Bank regulators play a crucial role in addressing these consequences by implementing stricter regulations, promoting transparency and accountability, protecting whistleblowers, and combating money laundering and corruption. By doing so, they can contribute to a more equitable and stable financial system that benefits society as a whole.

Case Studies: Financial Scandals and Widening Wealth Gap

Financial scandals in recent years have not only rocked the global economy but have also exposed the widening wealth gap, leading to significant consequences across various sectors. This subchapter delves into a series of case studies that shed light on the impact of these scandals and their implications for bank regulators, offshore tax havens, political fallout, legal actions, corporate transparency and accountability, social and economic inequality, whistleblowers, international relations, public perception, money laundering, and corruption.

One prominent case study is the Panama Papers scandal, which revealed the extent of tax evasion and money laundering facilitated by offshore tax havens. This scandal highlighted the urgent need for stricter regulations governing such havens and forced bank regulators to reassess their oversight mechanisms. The consequences for offshore tax havens were severe, as many faced international scrutiny and pressure to increase transparency.

Political fallout and resignations are also a significant outcome of financial scandals. When high-profile individuals, including politicians and public officials, are implicated in corruption or financial impropriety, public trust is eroded, leading to political turmoil and resignations. This subchapter explores the impact of such fallout on the stability of governments and the subsequent reforms in corporate transparency and accountability that are often initiated as a response.

Legal actions and prosecutions play a crucial role in holding individuals and institutions accountable for their involvement in financial scandals. This subchapter examines the legal consequences faced by those implicated and the reforms implemented to strengthen the legal framework surrounding financial crimes.

The widening wealth gap, exposed by these scandals, raises important social and economic inequality concerns. The case studies analyzed in this subchapter provide insights into how these scandals exacerbate existing inequalities and contribute to societal unrest. The role of whistleblowers and investigative journalism in uncovering these scandals is also examined, highlighting their crucial role in bringing such issues to light.

Furthermore, the effects of financial scandals on international relations and diplomacy cannot be overlooked. These scandals often strain relations between countries, as governments grapple with the fallout and implications for their diplomatic ties. Additionally, public perception of wealth and privilege is heavily influenced by these scandals, as they expose the true extent of corruption and unethical practices within the financial world.

Lastly, the subchapter explores the implications of financial scandals for money laundering and corruption. These scandals often reveal the flaws in anti-money laundering measures and expose the extent of systemic corruption within financial institutions.

Overall, this subchapter provides a comprehensive analysis of the case studies related to financial scandals and their wide-ranging impact on various sectors. It serves as a valuable resource for bank regulators seeking to understand the consequences of such scandals and the necessary reforms to prevent their recurrence.

Bernie Madoff Ponzi Scheme

The Bernie Madoff Ponzi Scheme is one of the most infamous financial scandals in recent history, shaking the global financial system to its core. This subchapter delves into the intricate web of deceit woven by Madoff and the far-reaching consequences it had on various aspects of the financial world. Addressed to bank regulators, it provides a comprehensive analysis of the impact on global financial regulations, consequences for offshore tax havens, political fallout and resignations, legal actions and prosecutions, reforms in corporate transparency and accountability, social and economic inequality exposed, the role of whistleblowers and investigative journalism, effects on international relations and diplomacy, public perception of wealth and privilege, and implications for money laundering and corruption.

Bernie Madoff, a former chairman of the NASDAQ stock exchange, orchestrated a Ponzi scheme that defrauded thousands of investors out of billions of dollars. His elaborate scheme involved using funds from new investors to pay returns to existing ones, creating an illusion of consistent profits. For years, Madoff managed to deceive regulators, auditors, and investors, leaving a trail of devastation in his wake.

The impact on global financial regulations was profound. Regulators worldwide were forced to reevaluate their oversight mechanisms and implement stricter regulations to prevent similar incidents. The Madoff scandal exposed significant loopholes that allowed such fraudulent activities to go undetected for an extended period.

Offshore tax havens also faced severe consequences. Madoff exploited these havens to launder money and hide his ill-gotten gains. As a result, there was increased scrutiny and pressure to crack down on tax havens and strengthen international cooperation to combat financial crimes.

The political fallout and resignations resulting from the Madoff scandal were significant. Several high-profile individuals and institutions were implicated, leading to a loss of public trust and credibility. Governments and regulatory bodies faced immense pressure to hold those responsible accountable and enact reforms to prevent future scandals.

Legal actions and prosecutions against Madoff and his associates were a key component of this scandal. The subchapter explores the legal proceedings and the resulting convictions, showcasing the importance of a robust legal system in combating financial crimes.

In response to the Madoff scandal, reforms in corporate transparency and accountability were initiated. Stricter reporting requirements, enhanced due diligence, and increased transparency became the norm, aiming to prevent similar fraudulent activities and protect investors.

The Madoff Ponzi scheme laid bare the social and economic inequality that exists within the financial system. The subchapter examines the widening wealth gap and the devastating impact the scandal had on individuals, charities, and businesses, highlighting the urgent need for systemic change.

Whistleblowers and investigative journalism played a crucial role in uncovering the Madoff scandal. Their efforts shed light on the depth of the deception and prompted further investigations. The subchapter explores their role in exposing financial wrongdoing and the importance of protecting whistleblowers.

The Madoff scandal had far-reaching effects on international relations and diplomacy. It strained relationships between countries, as governments demanded answers and sought justice for their affected citizens. Cooperation and coordination between nations became paramount in combating financial crimes.

Public perception of wealth and privilege was significantly influenced by the Madoff scandal. It exposed the dark underbelly of the financial world, highlighting the unethical practices and immense privileges enjoyed by a select few. This subchapter delves into the public outrage and calls for a more equitable financial system.

Lastly, the implications for money laundering and corruption are explored. Madoff's scheme revealed vulnerabilities in anti-money laundering processes, necessitating stronger measures to combat illicit financial flows and corrupt practices.

In conclusion, the Bernie Madoff Ponzi Scheme had a profound and lasting impact on various aspects of the financial world. This subchapter provides a comprehensive analysis of its implications, aiming to assist bank regulators in understanding the depth of the scandal and implementing appropriate measures to prevent future financial fraud.

Lehman Brothers Collapse

The collapse of Lehman Brothers in September 2008 sent shockwaves throughout the global financial system, leading to one of the most severe financial crises in modern history. This subchapter delves into the various dimensions of the Lehman Brothers collapse and its wide-ranging implications for bank regulators.

Impact on Global Financial Regulations:

The collapse of Lehman Brothers exposed glaring loopholes in global financial regulations. Bank regulators were forced to confront the inadequacies of existing frameworks, leading to a reevaluation of risk management practices, capital requirements, and the need for enhanced oversight and supervision. This chapter explores the reforms initiated in the aftermath of the collapse to prevent future financial crises.

Consequences for Offshore Tax Havens:

Lehman Brothers' collapse also shed light on the role of offshore tax havens in facilitating illicit financial activities. Bank regulators were compelled to examine the impact of these havens on the stability of the global financial system. This section analyzes the measures taken to address tax evasion, money laundering, and the need for greater transparency in offshore jurisdictions.

Political Fallout and Resignations:

The collapse of Lehman Brothers had far-reaching political consequences. This subchapter explores the public outrage, political backlash, and high-profile resignations that ensued. Bank regulators were faced with the challenge of restoring public trust in the financial system and holding accountable those responsible for the crisis.

Legal Actions and Prosecutions:

In the wake of the Lehman Brothers collapse, there were calls for justice and accountability. This section investigates the legal actions and prosecutions that followed, including investigations into potential fraud, insider trading, and regulatory failures. Bank regulators played a crucial role in ensuring that those responsible for the collapse faced appropriate legal consequences.

Reforms in Corporate Transparency and Accountability:

The collapse of Lehman Brothers highlighted the need for greater transparency and accountability in corporate governance. Bank regulators were at the forefront of efforts to implement reforms that would prevent similar failures in the future. This chapter explores the changes made to corporate governance frameworks and the role of bank regulators in enforcing these reforms.

Social and Economic Inequality Exposed:

The collapse of Lehman Brothers exposed the deep-seated social and economic inequalities that existed within the financial system. Bank regulators were confronted with the need to address these disparities and ensure a more inclusive and equitable financial system. This section examines the measures taken to mitigate social and economic inequality.

Role of Whistleblowers and Investigative Journalism:

Whistleblowers and investigative journalists played a crucial role in uncovering the misconduct and risky practices that contributed to the collapse of Lehman Brothers. This subchapter explores their efforts and the impact they had on exposing wrongdoing within the financial industry. Bank regulators were compelled to listen to and protect whistleblowers while strengthening their own investigative capacities.

Effects on International Relations and Diplomacy:

The collapse of Lehman Brothers had significant implications for international relations and diplomacy. This section examines how the crisis strained global cooperation, affected diplomatic relations, and influenced international negotiations on financial regulations. Bank regulators were tasked with rebuilding trust and fostering collaboration among nations.

Public Perception of Wealth and Privilege:

The collapse of Lehman Brothers shattered the illusion of invincibility surrounding Wall Street and the wealthy elite. This subchapter investigates the profound impact the crisis had on public perception of wealth and privilege. Bank regulators were faced with the challenge of rebuilding trust and restoring confidence in the financial sector.

Implications for Money Laundering and Corruption:

The collapse of Lehman Brothers exposed vulnerabilities in the financial system that facilitated money laundering and corruption. This section explores the measures taken by bank regulators to combat these illicit activities and safeguard the integrity of the financial system.

In conclusion, the collapse of Lehman Brothers had far-reaching consequences for bank regulators and the global financial system. This subchapter provides an in-depth analysis of the impact on global financial regulations, consequences for offshore tax havens, political fallout and resignations, legal actions and prosecutions, reforms in corporate transparency and accountability, social and economic inequality exposed, role of whistleblowers and investigative journalism, effects on international relations and diplomacy, public perception of wealth and privilege, and implications for money laundering and corruption. Bank regulators must learn from the lessons of the Lehman Brothers collapse to prevent future financial crises and foster a more stable and equitable financial system.

Addressing Social and Economic Inequality

In recent years, the world has witnessed a series of financial scandals that have not only rocked the global economy but also exposed the deep-rooted social and economic inequality that exists within our societies. This subchapter delves into the various aspects of this issue and explores the implications for bank regulators.

One of the key impacts of these financial scandals has been on global financial regulations. The revelations of corruption, money laundering, and tax evasion have highlighted the loopholes and weaknesses in the existing regulatory frameworks. Bank regulators must take note of these shortcomings and work towards strengthening the regulations to prevent such scandals from occurring in the future.

Furthermore, these scandals have also shed light on the consequences for offshore tax havens. These havens have long been used as a means to evade taxes and hide illicit funds. The revelations have resulted in increased scrutiny and pressure on these tax havens, leading to calls for stricter regulations and cooperation between countries to combat tax evasion effectively.

The political fallout and resignations that have followed these scandals have had a significant impact on the global financial landscape. The public's trust in financial institutions and regulators has been severely eroded, and there is a growing demand for accountability and transparency. Bank regulators must address these concerns by implementing reforms that promote corporate transparency and accountability.

The legal actions and prosecutions that arise from these scandals are vital in ensuring justice is served. Bank regulators need to work closely with law enforcement agencies to ensure that those responsible for these financial crimes are held accountable. This will help restore public trust and send a strong message that such behavior will not be tolerated.

Social and economic inequality has been laid bare by these scandals. The wealth and privilege enjoyed by a select few have been contrasted with the struggles faced by the majority. Bank regulators must recognize the role they play in addressing this inequality and work towards creating a more equitable financial system.

Whistleblowers and investigative journalism have played a crucial role in exposing these scandals. Their bravery and dedication should be commended, and bank regulators should establish mechanisms to protect and encourage whistleblowers. This will not only help uncover future wrongdoing but also foster a culture of integrity within the financial industry.

The effects of these scandals on international relations and diplomacy cannot be ignored. Countries have had to reassess their relationships with offshore tax havens and take a stand against money laundering and corruption. Bank regulators must actively participate in these discussions and collaborate with their global counterparts to develop a coordinated response.

The public perception of wealth and privilege has also been significantly impacted. These scandals have highlighted the vast disparities in income and the ways in which the wealthy can manipulate the system to their advantage. Bank regulators need to address this perception by actively working towards creating a fair and inclusive financial system.

Lastly, the implications for money laundering and corruption cannot be underestimated. These scandals have exposed the vulnerabilities that exist within the global financial system, and bank regulators must take immediate action to strengthen anti-money laundering measures and improve transparency.

In conclusion, the revelations of financial scandals have had far-reaching consequences for bank regulators. Addressing social and economic inequality is a critical aspect of this process, and regulators must play a proactive role in implementing reforms, promoting transparency, and fostering a culture of integrity within the financial industry. By doing so, they can help restore public trust and ensure a more equitable and stable global financial system.

Chapter 7: Role of Whistleblowers and Investigative Journalism

The Importance of Whistleblowers in Exposing Financial Scandals

In the world of finance, where vast sums of money change hands and intricate transactions take place, the potential for corruption and fraud is ever-present. This is why whistleblowers play a crucial role in exposing financial scandals and ensuring transparency and accountability in the global financial system. In this subchapter, we will explore the significance of whistleblowers and their impact on various aspects of the financial world.

One of the key areas where whistleblowers have a profound effect is on global financial regulations. By exposing wrongdoing and illegal activities, whistleblowers provide regulators with invaluable information that helps them identify and address gaps in the existing regulatory framework. Without whistleblowers, regulators would be left in the dark, making it extremely difficult to enforce regulations effectively and prevent future financial scandals from occurring.

Whistleblowers also have significant consequences for offshore tax havens. These tax havens often enable individuals and corporations to evade taxes and engage in illicit financial activities. Whistleblowers, armed with insider knowledge, can expose the intricate web of offshore accounts and transactions, leading to increased scrutiny and regulation of these tax havens. This, in turn, helps governments recoup lost tax revenue and reduces the incentives for individuals and corporations to engage in tax evasion.

The exposure of financial scandals through whistleblowers often leads to political fallout and resignative. When the public becomes aware of corruption and fraud within financial institutions, there is a loss of trust and confidence in those responsible for overseeing these institutions. As a result, politicians and high-ranking officials often face public pressure to take action, which can lead to resignations, firings, and even criminal prosecutions.

Legal actions and prosecutions are another consequence of whistleblowers' revelations. Whistleblowers often provide evidence that can be used in criminal investigations, leading to the prosecution of individuals involved in financial scandals. This not only holds wrongdoers accountable for their actions but also serves as a deterrent to others who may be tempted to engage in similar activities.

Reforms in corporate transparency and accountability are also a direct result of whistleblowers' contributions. When financial scandals are exposed, there is a heightened awareness of the need for increased transparency and accountability within corporations. This often leads to new regulations and policies that require companies to disclose more information about their financial activities, ensuring that shareholders and the public have a clearer understanding of their operations.

Furthermore, whistleblowers and investigative journalism play a vital role in uncovering social and economic inequalities that are often perpetuated by financial scandals. By exposing the unethical practices of powerful institutions, whistleblowers shed light on the mechanisms that contribute to these inequalities, prompting public discussions and calls for change.

The effects of whistleblowers' revelations can extend beyond national borders, impacting international relations and diplomacy. Financial scandals often involve cross-border transactions and interactions with foreign entities. When these scandals are exposed, they can strain diplomatic relationships and lead to increased scrutiny and regulation of financial activities between countries.

Whistleblowers also bring attention to the public perception of wealth and privilege. Financial scandals often involve the abuse of power by the wealthy and well-connected. When these scandals come to light, they expose the stark contrast between the privileged few and the rest of society, leading to increased scrutiny and demands for a fairer distribution of wealth.

Lastly, the exposure of financial scandals through whistleblowers has significant implications for money laundering and corruption. Whistleblowers often reveal the intricate networks and methods used to launder money and engage in corrupt practices. This information is vital for law enforcement agencies and governments in their efforts to combat money laundering and corruption.

In conclusion, whistleblowers play a crucial role in exposing financial scandals and bringing transparency to the global financial system. Their contributions have far-reaching effects, from impacting global financial regulations to uncovering social and economic inequalities. Whistleblowers are the catalysts for change, prompting legal actions, reforms, and increased scrutiny of financial activities. Their courage and commitment to upholding integrity and accountability should be acknowledged and protected, as they are instrumental in creating a more transparent and just financial world.

Whistleblower Protection Laws and Policies

In recent years, financial scandals have shaken the global economy, leading to a profound reevaluation of existing regulatory frameworks. As bank regulators, it is crucial to understand the impact of these scandals on global financial regulations and the subsequent need for robust whistleblower protection laws and policies.

Whistleblowers play a vital role in exposing corporate wrongdoing and promoting transparency in the financial sector. Their courage in coming forward with evidence of illegal activities has the potential to prevent widespread financial crises, protect investors, and restore public trust. However, without adequate protection, whistleblowers face significant risks, including retaliation, job loss, and even legal consequences. To ensure the effectiveness of their contributions, it is essential to implement comprehensive whistleblower protection laws and policies.

The consequences of financial scandals extend beyond the boundaries of any single nation. Offshore tax havens, often used as tools for illicit financial activities, have come under intense scrutiny. The exposure of these havens and the subsequent crackdown on tax evasion highlight the need for international cooperation in combating financial crimes. Whistleblower protection laws should not only be enforced domestically but also extend across borders, allowing individuals to report wrongdoing without fear of reprisals.

The political fallout and resignations that follow financial scandals underscore the urgency of implementing whistleblower protection laws and policies. When top executives and government officials are implicated in corruption or fraud, public trust in institutions is severely eroded. Whistleblowers provide a necessary check on the abuse of power, ensuring that those responsible are held accountable. By protecting whistleblowers, regulators can help restore faith in financial systems and prevent the recurrence of such scandals.

Legal actions and prosecutions are crucial in addressing financial crimes, but they heavily rely on the information provided by whistleblowers. Whistleblower protection laws encourage individuals to come forward with evidence, strengthening the legal case against wrongdoers. Without such protections, potential whistleblowers may hesitate, fearing personal and professional repercussions. By safeguarding their rights, regulators can effectively gather evidence and bring perpetrators to justice.

The need for reforms in corporate transparency and accountability is another critical aspect highlighted by financial scandals. Whistleblowers often shed light on unethical practices, prompting regulatory bodies to introduce stricter reporting requirements and corporate governance guidelines. By protecting whistleblowers, regulators can foster a culture of accountability and transparency, minimizing the likelihood of future financial scandals.

The role of whistleblowers and investigative journalism in exposing financial crimes cannot be overstated. Journalists often rely on information provided by whistleblowers to uncover corruption and illicit activities. Whistleblower protection laws and policies ensure that journalists can work without fear of legal repercussions or intimidation, enabling them to fulfill their role as watchdogs of society.

Financial scandals have far-reaching implications for international relations and diplomacy. When high-profile individuals or companies are implicated in illicit activities, it can strain relationships between nations. Whistleblower protection laws can facilitate the sharing of crucial information between countries, strengthening cooperation and enhancing the effectiveness of global efforts to combat financial crimes.

The public perception of wealth and privilege is also heavily influenced by financial scandals. When individuals in positions of power are shown to be engaged in illegal activities, it reinforces the perception of a rigged system that benefits the few at the expense of the many. Whistleblower protection laws empower individuals to challenge this perception, ensuring that justice prevails and restoring faith in the fairness of financial systems.

Finally, financial scandals have significant implications for money laundering and corruption. Whistleblowers are often at the forefront of exposing these illicit practices, providing invaluable information to regulatory bodies. By protecting whistleblowers, regulators can effectively address money laundering and corruption, safeguarding the integrity of the global financial system.

In conclusion, the importance of whistleblower protection laws and policies cannot be emphasized enough in the aftermath of financial scandals. By providing legal protection and support to whistleblowers, regulators can promote transparency, accountability, and integrity in the global financial sector. The consequences of failing to protect whistleblowers are severe, ranging from perpetuating financial crimes to eroding public trust. It is therefore imperative that bank regulators prioritize the implementation of comprehensive whistleblower protection laws and policies to prevent future financial scandals and promote a more just and transparent global financial system.

Investigative Journalism and Its Impact on Financial Scandals

In recent years, investigative journalism has played a significant role in exposing and unraveling complex financial scandals that have shaken the global economy. This subchapter will delve into the vital role played by investigative journalism in unearthing financial scandals, its impact on various aspects of the global financial landscape, and the consequences that have ensued.

Investigative journalism has had a profound impact on global financial regulations. Through in-depth investigations, journalists have uncovered loopholes, regulatory gaps, and instances of regulatory capture that have allowed financial scandals to occur. These revelations have prompted bank regulators to take a closer look at existing regulations and enact reforms to close these gaps, ensuring greater transparency and accountability in the financial sector.

Furthermore, investigative journalism has shed light on the consequences of offshore tax havens. Through meticulous investigations, journalists have exposed the intricate web of offshore tax havens and their role in facilitating tax evasion and money laundering. This has prompted regulators to tighten regulations and crack down on these havens, reducing their effectiveness as tax evasion tools and increasing international cooperation to combat offshore tax evasion.

The political fallout and subsequent resignations that often follow financial scandals have also been influenced by investigative journalism. Journalists have brought to light the involvement of politicians and government officials in these scandals, leading to public outrage and demands for accountability. As a result, politicians implicated in financial scandals have faced resignations, investigations, and legal actions, demonstrating the power of investigative journalism in holding individuals in positions of power accountable for their actions.

Legal actions and prosecutions against those involved in financial scandals have been bolstered by the evidence provided by investigative journalists. Journalists have acted as whistleblowers, providing crucial information to law enforcement agencies and regulatory bodies, enabling them to build strong cases against perpetrators of financial crimes.

Reforms in corporate transparency and accountability have also been a direct result of investigative journalism. Journalists have exposed the lack of transparency and unethical practices within corporations, leading to calls for reforms that require greater disclosure, accountability, and oversight.

The social and economic inequality exposed by investigative journalism has sparked public discourse and demands for change. By highlighting the vast disparities between the wealthy and the average citizen, journalists have prompted discussions on income inequality, fair distribution of resources, and the need for systemic change.

Whistleblowers have played a crucial role in bringing financial scandals to light, often with the assistance of investigative journalists. The role of whistleblowers and the symbiotic relationship they share with investigative journalism cannot be overstated. Whistleblowers provide insider information that journalists can investigate and verify, leading to the exposure of financial wrongdoing.

Furthermore, the effects of financial scandals on international relations and diplomacy are significant. Investigative journalism has exposed the involvement of foreign entities in financial scandals, straining diplomatic relations and prompting cross-border investigations and cooperation.

The public perception of wealth and privilege has been greatly impacted by investigative journalism. Journalists have exposed the lavish lifestyles and questionable practices of the wealthy elite, leading to a shift in public sentiment towards wealth and privilege. This has resulted in public demands for increased regulation and accountability for the wealthy.

Lastly, the implications for money laundering and corruption are substantial. Investigative journalism has exposed the mechanisms and networks used for money laundering, leading to increased efforts to combat these illicit activities and strengthen anti-corruption measures.

In conclusion, investigative journalism has had a profound impact on financial scandals, influencing global financial regulations, exposing offshore tax havens, triggering political fallout and resignations, leading to legal actions and prosecutions, driving reforms in corporate transparency and accountability, exposing social and economic inequality, highlighting the role of whistleblowers, affecting international relations and diplomacy, shaping public perception of wealth and privilege, and combatting money laundering and corruption. The power of investigative journalism cannot be underestimated in its ability to uncover financial wrongdoing and hold those responsible accountable for their actions.

Case Studies: Whistleblowers and Investigative Journalism Uncovering Scandals

In the realm of financial scandals, whistleblowers and investigative journalism play a pivotal role in uncovering the truth and exposing corruption. This subchapter delves into the intriguing case studies that highlight the significant impact of whistleblowers and investigative journalism on global financial regulations, offshore tax havens, political fallout, legal actions, corporate transparency, social and economic inequality, international relations, public perception, and implications for money laundering and corruption.

One such case study involves the infamous Panama Papers leak in 2016. The leak, made possible by an anonymous whistleblower, exposed a vast network of offshore tax havens and illicit financial activities involving prominent politicians, businesspeople, and celebrities. The revelation sent shockwaves across the globe, leading to a wave of regulatory scrutiny and international cooperation to combat tax evasion and money laundering.

Another notable case study involves the whistleblower Edward Snowden, who exposed the extensive surveillance programs carried out by intelligence agencies. Snowden's revelations sparked a global debate on privacy rights, government surveillance, and the role of technology companies in protecting user data. The scandal prompted reforms in corporate transparency and accountability, as companies faced increasing pressure to safeguard user privacy and disclose their cooperation with government surveillance programs.

The role of whistleblowers and investigative journalism in exposing corporate fraud and corruption is also exemplified by the Enron scandal. Through meticulous investigative reporting, journalists uncovered a web of deceit and accounting manipulations that led to the collapse of one of the largest energy companies in the United States. The scandal resulted in legal actions and prosecutions against top executives, as well as a renewed focus on corporate governance and financial reporting standards.

These case studies demonstrate the crucial role whistleblowers and investigative journalism play in holding corporations and governments accountable. Their efforts have led to significant reforms in global financial regulations, prompting increased transparency and stricter enforcement of anti-corruption measures. Moreover, the exposure of social and economic inequality has fueled public outrage and demands for a fairer distribution of wealth and opportunities.

The impact of whistleblowers and investigative journalism extends beyond national boundaries, affecting international relations and diplomacy. The uncovering of illicit financial activities and corruption scandals has strained diplomatic relations between countries, as governments face pressure to take action against those involved. The public perception of wealth and privilege has also been deeply affected, with increased scrutiny on the lifestyles and actions of the wealthy elite.

Furthermore, these case studies highlight the implications for money laundering and corruption. Whistleblowers and investigative journalists play a critical role in identifying and exposing illicit financial flows and corrupt practices, enabling authorities to take action and strengthen anti-money laundering measures.

In conclusion, the case studies presented in this subchapter emphasize the indispensable role of whistleblowers and investigative journalism in uncovering financial scandals and driving much-needed reforms. Their efforts have had far-reaching consequences, impacting global financial regulations, offshore tax havens, political dynamics, legal actions, corporate transparency, social and economic inequality, international relations, public perception, and the fight against money laundering and corruption. Bank regulators must recognize and support these whistleblowers and journalists as key allies in their pursuit of a fair and transparent financial system.

Chapter 8: Effects on International Relations and Diplomacy

Diplomatic Fallout from Financial Scandals

Financial scandals have far-reaching consequences that extend beyond national borders and impact international relations and diplomacy. This subchapter explores the diplomatic fallout resulting from these scandals and highlights the implications for global financial regulations, offshore tax havens, and international relations.

Financial scandals erode trust and confidence in the global financial system, leading to increased scrutiny and stricter regulations. Bank regulators play a crucial role in restoring stability and trust in the aftermath of these scandals. The exposure of widespread financial malpractices prompts regulators to reassess existing regulations and implement reforms to prevent similar incidents in the future.

One significant area affected by financial scandals is offshore tax havens. These scandals shed light on the role of these havens in facilitating tax evasion and money laundering. As a result, there is mounting pressure on regulators to crack down on these jurisdictions and enforce stricter regulations to ensure transparency and accountability.

The political fallout and resignations that follow financial scandals have profound implications for governments and their leaders. Public trust in political institutions is severely undermined, and citizens demand accountability from their elected officials. This can lead to political instability and the rise of populist movements.

Legal actions and prosecutions are often pursued in the wake of financial scandals. Regulators work closely with law enforcement agencies to hold individuals and corporations accountable for their actions. This sends a strong message that financial crimes will not go unpunished, and it serves as a deterrent for future wrongdoing.

Reforms in corporate transparency and accountability are another consequence of financial scandals. Regulators push for greater disclosure requirements and stricter corporate governance standards to prevent fraudulent practices. This ensures that corporations are held responsible for their actions and reduces the potential for future scandals.

Financial scandals expose the social and economic inequality that exists within societies. The public becomes acutely aware of the vast wealth disparities and the privileges enjoyed by the elite. This fuels resentment and can lead to social unrest if not addressed effectively by regulators and policymakers.

Whistleblowers and investigative journalism play a critical role in uncovering financial scandals. Their contributions are invaluable in holding corporations and individuals accountable for their actions. Regulators must create an environment that protects whistleblowers and encourages investigative journalism to ensure transparency and prevent future scandals.

The effects of financial scandals on international relations and diplomacy cannot be underestimated. These scandals damage the reputation of countries involved and strain diplomatic ties. Regulators must work collaboratively with their international counterparts to restore trust and cooperation in the global financial system.

Public perception of wealth and privilege is significantly influenced by financial scandals. These incidents highlight the excesses of the wealthy and powerful, which can lead to public outrage and demands for greater fairness and equality. Regulators must address these concerns and ensure that the financial system benefits all, not just the privileged few.

Finally, financial scandals have profound implications for money laundering and corruption. Regulators must strengthen their efforts to combat these illicit activities and implement robust anti-money laundering measures. This requires international cooperation and coordination to effectively tackle these global issues.

In conclusion, financial scandals have wide-ranging impacts on global financial regulations, offshore tax havens, international relations, and public perception. Bank regulators play a critical role in mitigating the diplomatic fallout from these scandals and implementing necessary reforms to prevent future incidents.

International Cooperation against Financial Crimes

Financial crimes have become a global concern, transcending borders and posing significant threats to the stability of the global financial system. In response to this challenge, international cooperation has emerged as a vital tool in the fight against such crimes. This subchapter will delve into the importance of international cooperation in combating financial crimes, the various initiatives that have been undertaken, and the impact on global financial regulations.

The consequences of financial scandals and the subsequent fallout have highlighted the urgent need for collaboration among nations to address these issues effectively. The interconnectedness of the global economy means that illicit funds can easily move across jurisdictions, evading detection and prosecution. As a result, bank regulators worldwide have recognized the necessity of working together to share information, intelligence, and best practices to combat financial crimes.

One of the key areas where international cooperation has played a crucial role is in tackling offshore tax havens. These havens have long been associated with facilitating tax evasion and money laundering. Through international cooperation, regulators have been able to crack down on these havens, implementing stricter regulations and enhancing transparency to prevent the abuse of these jurisdictions.

The political fallout and high-profile resignations resulting from financial scandals have shaken public trust in financial institutions and regulatory bodies. International cooperation has provided a platform for sharing lessons learned and implementing reforms to restore confidence in the financial system. Through collaborative efforts, regulators have been able to hold accountable those responsible for financial crimes, ensuring that justice is served and serving as a deterrent for future wrongdoings.

Moreover, international cooperation has led to significant reforms in corporate transparency and accountability. Regulators have worked together to establish global standards for reporting financial transactions, enhancing due diligence requirements, and implementing measures to prevent money laundering and corruption. These reforms aim to create a more transparent and accountable corporate environment, minimizing the risk of financial crimes.

The role of whistleblowers and investigative journalism cannot be understated in uncovering financial crimes. International cooperation has provided a platform for whistleblowers to come forward and share crucial information, resulting in the exposure of numerous scandals. Investigative journalists have also played a vital role in bringing these crimes to light, prompting regulatory action and initiating legal proceedings.

The effects of financial scandals and the subsequent international cooperation have not been limited to the financial sector alone. These incidents have exposed the social and economic inequality prevalent in society, highlighting the privileges enjoyed by the wealthy and the adverse consequences faced by the less privileged. This realization has sparked public debates and calls for greater equality and fairness in the distribution of wealth.

Furthermore, international cooperation against financial crimes has had significant implications for international relations and diplomacy. Governments have collaborated to extradite individuals involved in financial crimes, developed mutual legal assistance treaties, and established joint task forces. These efforts have strengthened diplomatic ties and fostered trust among nations, paving the way for future cooperation in combating financial crimes.

The public perception of wealth and privilege has also been greatly influenced by financial scandals. The exposure of illicit financial activities has fueled public outrage and led to increased scrutiny of the wealthy and their privileged lifestyles. This heightened awareness has prompted demands for greater accountability and transparency from the wealthy elite, further pushing regulators to take action against financial crimes.

Finally, the fight against financial crimes has had significant implications for money laundering and corruption. International cooperation has enabled regulators to share intelligence, coordinate investigations, and implement measures to prevent and detect illicit financial activities. By working together, bank regulators have been able to disrupt money laundering networks and curb corruption, safeguarding the integrity of the global financial system.

In conclusion, international cooperation against financial crimes is crucial in today's interconnected world. The impact on global financial regulations, consequences for offshore tax havens, political fallout and resignations, legal actions and prosecutions, reforms in corporate transparency and accountability, social and economic inequality exposed, role of whistleblowers and investigative journalism, effects on international relations and diplomacy, public perception of wealth and privilege, and implications for money laundering and corruption all highlight the significance of collaborative efforts in combating financial crimes. Bank regulators must continue to strengthen international cooperation to effectively tackle these challenges and safeguard the global financial system.

Impact on Bilateral and Multilateral Relations

The far-reaching consequences of financial scandals extend beyond national borders, impacting bilateral and multilateral relations between countries. These scandals have the potential to strain diplomatic ties, disrupt international trade, and erode trust between nations. This subchapter sheds light on the various ways in which financial scandals have influenced global relations and the subsequent implications for bank regulators.

One of the key areas affected by financial scandals is the global financial regulatory framework. As scandals unfold, regulators are faced with the daunting task of reassessing existing regulations and implementing new measures to prevent similar occurrences in the future. The impact on global financial regulations is profound, as countries strive to harmonize their regulatory frameworks to enhance transparency and accountability in the banking sector.

Furthermore, financial scandals have exposed the role played by offshore tax havens in facilitating illicit financial activities. As a result, countries have faced mounting pressure to crack down on these tax havens and impose stricter regulations to prevent tax evasion and money laundering. Bilateral and multilateral discussions on this issue have become more prevalent, as countries seek to collaborate in combating offshore tax havens and promoting fair tax practices.

Political fallout and high-profile resignations are common consequences of financial scandals. These events can strain diplomatic relations, especially if high-level officials are implicated in the scandals. The subchapter explores the impact of such political fallout on bilateral and multilateral relations, highlighting instances where scandals have strained relations between countries and led to diplomatic tensions.

Legal actions and prosecutions resulting from financial scandals also have implications for international relations. Collaboration between law enforcement agencies across borders becomes crucial to bring perpetrators to justice. Bilateral and multilateral agreements on extradition and legal cooperation are often strengthened in the aftermath of financial scandals.

The exposure of corruption and money laundering through investigative journalism and whistleblowers has far-reaching consequences for international relations. These revelations can tarnish the reputation of countries involved and lead to strained diplomatic ties. The subchapter delves into case studies where the role of whistleblowers and investigative journalism has impacted diplomatic relations and prompted international cooperation in combating financial crimes.

In conclusion, financial scandals have a significant impact on bilateral and multilateral relations. They necessitate reforms in global financial regulations, intensify discussions on offshore tax havens, lead to political fallout and resignations, trigger legal actions and prosecutions, expose social and economic inequality, highlight the importance of whistleblowers and investigative journalism, affect international relations and diplomacy, shape public perception of wealth and privilege, and have implications for money laundering and corruption. Bank regulators must be aware of these consequences and work collaboratively to address the challenges posed by financial scandals on a global scale.

Case Studies: Political Consequences and Diplomatic Relations

In this subchapter, we will delve into several case studies that highlight the political consequences and diplomatic relations resulting from financial scandals. These case studies shed light on the far-reaching impact these scandals have had on global financial regulations, offshore tax havens, political fallout and resignations, legal actions and prosecutions, reforms in corporate transparency and accountability, social and economic inequality, whistleblowers and investigative journalism, international relations and diplomacy, public perception of wealth and privilege, and implications for money laundering and corruption.

One case study that stands out is the Panama Papers scandal. The leak of millions of documents from the law firm Mossack Fonseca exposed the widespread use of offshore tax havens by politicians, celebrities, and wealthy individuals around the world. This revelation had profound implications for global financial regulations, as regulators sought to tighten loopholes and prevent tax evasion on such a massive scale. The scandal also led to the resignation of several high-profile politicians and public officials, as their involvement in questionable financial practices came to light.

Another case study worth examining is the FIFA corruption scandal. This scandal exposed rampant corruption within the world's governing body for football, revealing how bribes and kickbacks influenced the awarding of hosting rights for major tournaments. The political fallout from this scandal was significant, with top FIFA officials being arrested and charged with corruption. Diplomatic relations between countries were strained as allegations of bribery and misconduct implicated officials from various nations. The fallout from this scandal also led to reforms in corporate transparency and accountability within FIFA, as well as a reevaluation of the public perception of wealth and privilege associated with the sport.

A third case study that highlights the political consequences and diplomatic relations resulting from financial scandals is the 1MDB scandal in Malaysia. This scandal involved the misappropriation of billions of dollars from a state investment fund, leading to widespread allegations of money laundering and corruption. The political fallout was immense, with the then Prime Minister of Malaysia facing pressure to resign amidst allegations of involvement in the scandal. Diplomatic relations were strained as investigations revealed the involvement of foreign politicians and businesspeople in the illicit activities surrounding 1MDB.

These case studies illustrate the wide-ranging effects that financial scandals can have on political systems and diplomatic relations. They underscore the need for robust global financial regulations, reforms in corporate transparency and accountability, and the crucial role played by whistleblowers and investigative journalism in exposing such wrongdoing. The consequences of these scandals extend far beyond mere legal actions and prosecutions, with implications for social and economic inequality, international relations, public perception, and the fight against money laundering and corruption. Bank regulators must be vigilant in their efforts to prevent and address such scandals, as they have the potential to undermine trust in financial systems and threaten the stability of global economies.

Chapter 9: Public Perception of Wealth and Privilege

Shifting Public Perception of Wealth and Privilege

In the wake of recent financial scandals, there has been a significant shift in public perception regarding wealth and privilege. The once-glamorized image of the ultra-rich has been tarnished, and society is now demanding greater transparency and accountability from those in positions of power. This subchapter explores the profound implications of this shifting public perception on various aspects of the global financial landscape.

One of the most notable impacts is the effect on global financial regulations. As public outrage grows, regulators are under increasing pressure to tighten oversight and close loopholes that allow for illicit financial activities. Governments around the world are facing mounting demands to crack down on offshore tax havens, which have long been associated with enabling tax evasion and money laundering. The public's newfound skepticism towards the wealthy elite has forced regulators to reevaluate their approach and implement more stringent measures to prevent future financial scandals.

The consequences for offshore tax havens are also significant. As public perception of wealth and privilege turns negative, individuals and corporations are facing greater scrutiny for their involvement in these tax havens. The revelations from recent scandals have exposed the extent of corruption and money laundering facilitated by these havens, leading to calls for their closure and increased international cooperation to combat illicit financial flows.

Moreover, the political fallout and resignations resulting from these scandals have created a sense of urgency for legal actions and prosecutions. The public demands justice for those responsible for the financial misconduct that has led to widespread economic inequalities. Governments and law enforcement agencies are under pressure to hold individuals and corporations accountable, ensuring that they face the consequences of their actions.

This shift in public perception has also sparked a demand for reforms in corporate transparency and accountability. Shareholders and investors are increasingly demanding greater disclosure and ethical practices from the companies they invest in. This has led to a push for increased corporate transparency, with calls for more robust reporting and oversight mechanisms to prevent future financial scandals.

In addition, the public's growing awareness of social and economic inequality has been magnified by the revelations of these scandals. The gap between the haves and have-nots has become even more evident, and there is a heightened sense of urgency to address this issue. The public is demanding that governments and regulators take action to address the systemic issues that perpetuate this inequality.

The role of whistleblowers and investigative journalism has also come into focus. The brave individuals who expose financial misconduct have become heroes in the eyes of the public. Their actions have shed light on the dark underbelly of the financial world and have played a crucial role in shifting public perception.

The effects of these financial scandals have extended beyond national borders, impacting international relations and diplomacy. Countries are reevaluating their relationships with offshore tax havens and demanding greater cooperation in combating money laundering and corruption. The public's perception of wealth and privilege has influenced diplomatic decisions, with nations prioritizing transparency and accountability in their dealings with other countries.

Finally, perhaps one of the most profound changes resulting from these scandals is the way the public perceives wealth and privilege. The once-romanticized notions of the ultra-rich have given way to skepticism and suspicion. There is a growing belief that wealth and privilege come at the expense of others and are often obtained through unethical means. This shift in perception has the potential to reshape societal values and priorities, influencing both individual behaviors and government policies.

Overall, the shifting public perception of wealth and privilege in the aftermath of financial scandals has far-reaching implications. From impacting global financial regulations and offshore tax havens to sparking legal actions, reforms in corporate transparency, and exposing social and economic inequality, the consequences are significant. The role of whistleblowers and investigative journalism, effects on international relations, and implications for money laundering and corruption are all critical factors that must be considered in this evolving landscape. As bank regulators, it is crucial to understand and respond to these shifting perceptions to rebuild public trust and ensure a more equitable and transparent financial system.

Impact of Financial Scandals on Public Opinion

Financial scandals have the ability to shake public trust in institutions, particularly in the banking sector. These scandals can have far-reaching consequences on various aspects of society, leading to a significant impact on public opinion. Understanding the dynamics of this impact is crucial for bank regulators in order to address the concerns and restore public confidence in the financial system.

One of the key areas affected by financial scandals is global financial regulations. When scandals occur, they often expose weaknesses in existing regulations, prompting regulators to examine and revise their frameworks. Public opinion plays a crucial role in this process, as public outrage and demand for stricter regulations can pressure regulators to take action. The impact of financial scandals on global financial regulations is therefore twofold: it reveals regulatory gaps and triggers reforms driven by public opinion.

Financial scandals also have significant consequences for offshore tax havens. When scandals uncover illegal or unethical practices involving offshore accounts, public opinion turns against these havens. The exposure of tax evasion and money laundering schemes erodes public trust not only in individual banks but also in the jurisdictions that facilitate these illicit activities. As a result, regulators are pushed to crack down on offshore tax havens, imposing stricter regulations to prevent further abuse.

Furthermore, political fallout and resignations often accompany financial scandals. Public opinion plays a pivotal role in determining the fate of politicians and corporate leaders involved in these scandals. When public trust is shattered, individuals are held accountable through legal actions and prosecutions. The public demands justice, and regulators must respond by ensuring that those responsible for the scandals face appropriate consequences.

Financial scandals also shed light on the need for reforms in corporate transparency and accountability. When public opinion is swayed by these scandals, there is increased pressure for companies to be more transparent in their operations and disclose potential risks. Regulators are then tasked with implementing measures that promote corporate responsibility and prevent future scandals.

The exposure of financial scandals also brings socio-economic inequality to the forefront. Public opinion often focuses on the disparity between the wealthy elite and the average citizen. Scandals involving fraud, embezzlement, or unethical practices reinforce the perception that the privileged few are benefiting at the expense of the majority. This heightened awareness of inequality can lead to social unrest and demands for broader reforms to address the wealth gap.

Whistleblowers and investigative journalism play a crucial role in uncovering financial scandals. When public opinion is shaped by the bravery of whistleblowers and the efforts of investigative journalists, there is increased pressure on regulators to protect and support these individuals. Their role in exposing corruption and holding institutions accountable cannot be overstated.

The effects of financial scandals extend beyond national borders, impacting international relations and diplomacy. When scandals involve multinational corporations or cross-border money laundering, public opinion can strain diplomatic relations between countries. Regulators must navigate these tensions and collaborate with international counterparts to address the transnational implications of financial scandals.

Public perception of wealth and privilege is often distorted by financial scandals. As scandals unfold, the public becomes more critical of the excessive wealth and privileges enjoyed by the elite. This scrutiny can lead to a shift in public opinion, with demands for greater transparency and fairness in the distribution of wealth.

Finally, financial scandals have severe implications for money laundering and corruption. Public opinion demands that regulators take decisive action to prevent illicit financial activities. This pressure can result in the strengthening of anti-money laundering measures and the prosecution of corrupt individuals. Regulators must respond by implementing reforms that address the weaknesses exposed by financial scandals and restore public trust in the financial system.

In conclusion, financial scandals have a profound impact on public opinion. The consequences reach far and wide, affecting global financial regulations, offshore tax havens, political dynamics, legal actions, corporate transparency, social and economic inequality, whistleblowers, international relations, public perception, and efforts to combat money laundering and corruption. Bank regulators must be attuned to these impacts and respond accordingly to restore public confidence in the financial system.

Populist Movements and Anti-Establishment Sentiments

In recent years, the rise of populist movements and anti-establishment sentiments has had a profound impact on global financial regulations. This subchapter explores the various consequences of these movements and sentiments, shedding light on how they have shaped the landscape of offshore tax havens, triggered political fallout and resignations, led to legal actions and prosecutions, prompted reforms in corporate transparency and accountability, exposed social and economic inequality, highlighted the role of whistleblowers and investigative journalism, affected international relations and diplomacy, influenced public perception of wealth and privilege, and intensified efforts to combat money laundering and corruption.

One of the key consequences of populist movements and anti-establishment sentiments has been their impact on offshore tax havens. These movements have exposed the extent of tax evasion and aggressive tax avoidance facilitated by these havens, prompting widespread calls for stricter regulations and increased transparency. Bank regulators have been at the forefront of these efforts, working to close loopholes and ensure that financial institutions are held accountable for their role in facilitating tax evasion.

The political fallout and resignations resulting from financial scandals have also been significant. Populist movements have capitalized on public anger and frustration towards the perceived corruption and cronyism within the establishment. As a result, there have been widespread calls for political accountability and demands for resignations from those implicated in financial wrongdoing. Bank regulators have been tasked with investigating these scandals and ensuring that those responsible are held legally and ethically accountable.

Furthermore, the exposure of financial scandals has prompted reforms in corporate transparency and accountability. Populist movements have highlighted the need for greater oversight and stricter regulations to prevent future abuses. Bank regulators have responded by implementing measures to enhance transparency, strengthen corporate governance, and promote responsible business practices.

The rise of populist movements has also brought to the forefront the issue of social and economic inequality. These movements have exposed the vast disparities in wealth and privilege, fueling public discontent and calls for more equitable economic systems. Bank regulators have been called upon to address these concerns by implementing policies that promote inclusive growth, reduce inequality, and ensure that financial systems work for the benefit of all.

The role of whistleblowers and investigative journalism cannot be overstated in uncovering financial scandals and holding the establishment accountable. Populist movements have rallied behind these individuals and organizations, recognizing their crucial role in exposing corruption and wrongdoing. Bank regulators have acknowledged the importance of protecting whistleblowers and facilitating investigative journalism to ensure transparency and accountability within the financial sector.

In addition to domestic consequences, the impact of populist movements and anti-establishment sentiments extends to international relations and diplomacy. The exposure of financial scandals has strained relationships between countries, with accusations of money laundering and corruption leading to diplomatic tensions. Bank regulators have had to navigate these complex dynamics, working to restore trust and cooperation between nations.

The public perception of wealth and privilege has also been influenced by populist movements. These movements have challenged the idea that wealth equates to merit or success, highlighting the role of privilege and connections in accumulating vast fortunes. Bank regulators have been tasked with addressing these concerns, working to restore public trust in the financial system and ensure that it serves the broader interests of society.

Finally, populist movements have intensified efforts to combat money laundering and corruption. The exposure of financial scandals has revealed the extent of illicit financial flows and the role of offshore tax havens in facilitating these activities. Bank regulators have been at the forefront of international initiatives to strengthen anti-money laundering measures, enhance financial transparency, and combat corruption.

In conclusion, the rise of populist movements and anti-establishment sentiments has had far-reaching consequences for global financial regulations. Bank regulators play a crucial role in addressing these consequences, working to enhance transparency, accountability, and fairness within the financial system. By responding effectively to the challenges posed by populist movements, bank regulators can help restore public trust and ensure a more stable and equitable financial landscape.

Examining the Long-Term Effects on Wealth Perception

In the aftermath of financial scandals, it is crucial for bank regulators to comprehensively analyze the long-term effects on wealth perception. This subchapter delves into the profound impact these scandals have on various aspects, such as global financial regulations, offshore tax havens, political fallout and resignations, legal actions and prosecutions, reforms in corporate transparency and accountability, social and economic inequality, the role of whistleblowers and investigative journalism, effects on international relations and diplomacy, public perception of wealth and privilege, as well as implications for money laundering and corruption.

The revelations of financial scandals often expose major gaps in global financial regulations. Bank regulators need to closely examine the loopholes that allowed these scandals to occur and assess the effectiveness of existing regulations. By learning from these incidents, regulators can strengthen financial frameworks, ensuring greater transparency, accountability, and stability.

Offshore tax havens, notorious for facilitating illicit financial activities, come under intense scrutiny in the wake of financial scandals. It is imperative for regulators to investigate how these tax havens were exploited and devise strategies to prevent future abuse. By collaborating with international partners, regulators can enhance cooperation and implement measures to combat tax evasion and money laundering.

The political fallout and resignations that follow financial scandals raise critical questions about the integrity of public officials and the efficacy of governance systems. Bank regulators must examine the systemic failures that allowed these scandals to occur and hold accountable those responsible. This subchapter will explore the legal actions and prosecutions initiated against individuals and organizations involved in financial wrongdoing, highlighting the importance of justice and deterrence.

Reforms in corporate transparency and accountability emerge as key priorities in the aftermath of financial scandals. Bank regulators should assess the adequacy of current reporting and disclosure requirements, urging corporations to adopt stronger measures to prevent fraud and corruption. Enhancing corporate governance practices will help restore public trust and confidence in the financial system.

Furthermore, financial scandals often expose the stark realities of social and economic inequality. Regulators must analyze how these scandals perpetuate inequality and devise strategies to mitigate its effects. By implementing policies that promote inclusive growth, regulators can address the root causes of wealth disparity and foster a more equitable society.

The role of whistleblowers and investigative journalism in uncovering financial scandals cannot be overstated. Bank regulators should recognize and protect the rights of whistleblowers, encouraging a culture of reporting wrongdoing. Additionally, regulators should collaborate with investigative journalists to enhance transparency and hold offenders accountable.

Financial scandals can have far-reaching implications for international relations and diplomacy. Regulators need to consider how these incidents impact diplomatic relationships, cross-border cooperation, and the reputation of the countries involved. By fostering international dialogue and cooperation, regulators can work towards preventing similar scandals in the future.

The public perception of wealth and privilege is profoundly affected by financial scandals. Regulators must address public concerns regarding excessive wealth accumulation, ensuring that the financial system operates in a manner that benefits society as a whole. By promoting fair wealth distribution and tackling systemic inequalities, regulators can restore public faith in the financial sector.

Finally, financial scandals have significant implications for money laundering and corruption. Regulators must closely examine the vulnerabilities exposed by these scandals and implement robust measures to prevent illicit financial activities. By strengthening anti-money laundering frameworks and enforcing stricter regulations, regulators can mitigate the risk of corruption and illicit financial flows.

In conclusion, examining the long-term effects on wealth perception is of utmost importance for bank regulators. By thoroughly analyzing the impact of financial scandals on various aspects, regulators can implement necessary reforms, strengthen global financial regulations, and restore public trust in the financial system.

Chapter 10: Implications for Money Laundering and Corruption

Link between Financial Scandals and Money Laundering

Money laundering has long been identified as a key component of financial scandals across the globe. In this subchapter, we will explore the intricate connection between financial scandals and money laundering, shedding light on the ways in which these two phenomena are interlinked and the implications they have on various aspects of society.

Financial scandals, characterized by fraudulent activities, misappropriation of funds, and the manipulation of financial systems, often provide the perfect breeding ground for money laundering. As illicit funds flow through complex networks, they are laundered to appear legitimate, obscuring their true origins and allowing criminals to benefit from the proceeds of their illegal activities.

The impact on global financial regulations cannot be understated. Financial scandals expose the weaknesses and loopholes in existing regulatory frameworks, prompting bank regulators to reassess and strengthen their oversight mechanisms. The revelation that these scandals are often facilitated by offshore tax havens further intensifies the need for stricter regulations to combat tax evasion and financial crime.

Political fallout and resignations are inevitable consequences of financial scandals. The revelation of corruption and unethical practices within the corridors of power erodes public trust in governments and their ability to effectively regulate the financial sector. As a result, politicians and high-ranking officials often face public outcry, leading to resignations and sometimes even criminal prosecutions.

Legal actions and prosecutions play a crucial role in holding individuals and corporations accountable for their involvement in financial scandals. The exposure of money laundering schemes within these scandals provides law enforcement agencies with vital evidence to pursue criminal charges against those responsible. These legal actions serve as a deterrent and send a clear message that financial crimes will not go unpunished.

Reforms in corporate transparency and accountability are another consequence of financial scandals. The public demand for greater transparency and ethical behavior from corporations grows stronger with each scandal. As a result, companies are forced to adopt measures that enhance their accountability and disclosure practices, aiming to restore trust among their stakeholders.

Financial scandals also expose the deep-rooted social and economic inequality within societies. As the public becomes more aware of the vast wealth disparities and the privileges enjoyed by the elite, there is an increased demand for a fairer distribution of wealth and opportunities. This growing awareness often sparks social movements and political pressure for greater equality and justice.

The role of whistleblowers and investigative journalism cannot be overstated in uncovering financial scandals and the money laundering activities associated with them. Whistleblowers, often driven by a sense of moral duty, play a critical role in exposing illicit practices, aiding law enforcement agencies, and triggering investigations. Investigative journalists, armed with their skills and determination, shed light on the intricate web of corruption, ensuring the public remains informed and engaged.

The effects of financial scandals and money laundering extend beyond national borders, impacting international relations and diplomacy. The revelation that illicit funds are often funneled through international financial systems strains diplomatic ties between countries. Cooperation and information sharing between nations become essential in the fight against money laundering and corruption.

Public perception of wealth and privilege is significantly influenced by financial scandals. The exposure of corrupt practices and the misuse of funds erode public trust in the wealthy and the privileged. This can lead to a shift in societal attitudes towards wealth accumulation, with a greater emphasis placed on ethical behavior and social responsibility.

Finally, financial scandals have far-reaching implications for money laundering and corruption. As regulators and law enforcement agencies close existing loopholes and enhance their ability to detect and prevent money laundering, criminals are forced to adapt their methods, leading to the evolution of increasingly sophisticated techniques. The fight against money laundering becomes an ongoing battle, requiring constant vigilance and collaboration between stakeholders.

In conclusion, the link between financial scandals and money laundering is undeniable. These two phenomena intertwine in a complex web of corruption, fraud, and illicit financial flows. The consequences of financial scandals are vast, impacting global financial regulations, offshore tax havens, political systems, legal actions, corporate transparency, social and economic inequality, whistleblowers, international relations, public perception, and the fight against money laundering and corruption. Recognizing and understanding this link is crucial for bank regulators in their quest to safeguard the integrity and stability of the financial system.

Role of Corruption in Facilitating Financial Scandals

Corruption has long been recognized as a significant factor in facilitating financial scandals around the world. In this subchapter, we will delve into the role corruption plays in these scandals, shedding light on its impact on global financial regulations, consequences for offshore tax havens, political fallout and resignations, legal actions and prosecutions, reforms in corporate transparency and accountability, social and economic inequality exposed, role of whistleblowers and investigative journalism, effects on international relations and diplomacy, public perception of wealth and privilege, and implications for money laundering and corruption.

Financial scandals are often fueled by the presence of corruption within the regulatory bodies responsible for overseeing the banking sector. When regulators are susceptible to bribery and other corrupt practices, they may turn a blind eye to suspicious activities, allowing illegal transactions to go unnoticed. This lack of oversight creates an environment ripe for financial malfeasance, enabling scandals to flourish.

Moreover, corruption plays a central role in the existence and success of offshore tax havens. These havens thrive on secrecy and opacity, providing a safe haven for individuals and corporations to hide their ill-gotten wealth and evade taxes. Corrupt officials, both within the tax havens and in other countries, often facilitate these activities by accepting bribes and turning a blind eye to illicit financial flows.

The consequences of financial scandals are not limited to regulatory failures or tax evasion. They often result in political fallout and resignations, as public trust in the system is shattered. Scandals expose the deep-rooted corruption within governments and financial institutions, leading to widespread calls for accountability and reform. Legal actions and prosecutions are initiated to hold those responsible accountable, but corruption can hinder the progress of these efforts, with influential individuals evading justice through their corrupt connections.

The revelation of financial scandals also highlights the urgent need for reforms in corporate transparency and accountability. Transparency and accountability mechanisms must be strengthened to prevent corruption and illicit financial activities. This includes implementing stricter regulations and ensuring that corporate entities are held to account for their actions.

Financial scandals also expose the stark social and economic inequality that exists within societies. These scandals often involve the misappropriation of public funds or the exploitation of vulnerable populations, exacerbating existing inequalities and widening the wealth gap. This revelation sparks public outrage and demands for greater equality and justice.

Whistleblowers and investigative journalism play a crucial role in uncovering financial scandals. These individuals and organizations risk their safety and livelihoods to expose corruption and illicit activities. Their efforts contribute to the public's understanding of the scandal and provide evidence for legal actions and prosecutions.

The effects of financial scandals extend beyond national borders, impacting international relations and diplomacy. Scandals involving offshore tax havens strain diplomatic relations between countries, as allegations of complicity and facilitation of corruption arise. Cooperation between nations becomes essential to combat money laundering and corruption on a global scale.

Public perception of wealth and privilege is significantly influenced by financial scandals. Scandals involving the elite and powerful erode public trust and raise questions about the fairness of the economic system. This leads to a reevaluation of societal values and a demand for more equitable distribution of wealth and opportunities.

Lastly, financial scandals have profound implications for money laundering and corruption. These scandals expose the vulnerabilities within the global financial system and highlight the need for stronger anti-money laundering measures. Governments and regulatory bodies must collaborate to develop robust frameworks to prevent and detect money laundering and corruption.

In conclusion, corruption plays a pivotal role in facilitating financial scandals. It undermines global financial regulations, enables offshore tax havens, leads to political fallout and resignations, hampers legal actions and prosecutions, necessitates reforms in corporate transparency and accountability, exposes social and economic inequality, highlights the importance of whistleblowers and investigative journalism, affects international relations and diplomacy, shapes public perception of wealth and privilege, and underscores the need to combat money laundering and corruption. Addressing corruption at its core is crucial to mitigating the occurrence and impact of financial scandals.

Strengthening Anti-Money Laundering Measures

In the wake of recent financial scandals that have rocked the global economy, it has become imperative for bank regulators to take immediate action and strengthen anti-money laundering measures. The consequences of these scandals have been far-reaching, impacting global financial regulations, offshore tax havens, political stability, legal actions and prosecutions, corporate transparency and accountability, social and economic inequality, international relations and diplomacy, public perception of wealth and privilege, as well as implications for money laundering and corruption.

One of the most significant impacts of these scandals has been on global financial regulations. The loopholes and weaknesses in the existing regulatory framework have been exposed, necessitating urgent reforms to prevent further abuse. Bank regulators must collaborate with international organizations, such as the Financial Action Task Force (FATF), to develop robust and comprehensive anti-money laundering policies. These policies should include stringent know-your-customer (KYC) procedures, enhanced due diligence, and the implementation of advanced technological solutions, such as artificial intelligence and blockchain, to detect and prevent illicit financial activities.

The consequences for offshore tax havens have also been severe. These jurisdictions, historically known for their lax regulations and secrecy laws, have come under intense scrutiny. Bank regulators must work closely with these tax havens to ensure transparency and cooperation in sharing financial information. The establishment of a centralized global database, where information on beneficial ownership and financial transactions can be accessed by authorized agencies, would be a crucial step towards combating money laundering.

Furthermore, the political fallout and resignations resulting from these scandals have highlighted the urgent need for legal actions and prosecutions. Bank regulators must collaborate with law enforcement agencies to ensure that those responsible for facilitating money laundering and corruption are held accountable. This requires strengthening of the legal frameworks, providing sufficient resources to investigation agencies, and ensuring swift and effective legal proceedings.

Reforms in corporate transparency and accountability are also essential to restore public trust in the financial system. Bank regulators must enforce stricter reporting requirements, including the disclosure of ultimate beneficial owners of companies. Additionally, the role of whistleblowers and investigative journalism cannot be undermined. Bank regulators should provide protection and incentives for individuals who expose financial misconduct, and foster a culture of transparency and accountability within the industry.

The social and economic inequality exposed by these scandals calls for immediate action. Bank regulators should work towards creating a more inclusive financial system, where the benefits are distributed equitably. This includes promoting financial literacy, enhancing access to banking services for underprivileged communities, and implementing measures to prevent tax evasion and illicit financial flows.

The effects on international relations and diplomacy cannot be ignored. Bank regulators must collaborate with their counterparts in other jurisdictions to ensure consistent implementation and enforcement of anti-money laundering measures. This requires fostering strong bilateral and multilateral relationships, sharing of intelligence and best practices, and promoting international cooperation in combating financial crimes.

The public perception of wealth and privilege has been significantly impacted by these scandals. Bank regulators must address this by promoting transparency and fairness in the financial system. This includes ensuring that the wealthy and powerful are not immune to prosecution, and that everyone is subject to the same rules and regulations.

Lastly, the implications for money laundering and corruption cannot be underestimated. Bank regulators must adopt a proactive approach, constantly evolving and adapting their strategies to stay ahead of sophisticated criminals. This includes investing in advanced technology, training personnel, and fostering a culture of compliance within financial institutions.

In conclusion, the recent financial scandals have exposed significant weaknesses in the global financial system. Bank regulators must take immediate action to strengthen anti-money laundering measures, in order to restore public trust, ensure global financial stability, and combat money laundering and corruption effectively. By collaborating with international organizations, implementing robust regulatory frameworks, and promoting transparency and accountability, bank regulators can play a pivotal role in preventing future financial scandals and safeguarding the integrity of the global economy.

Global Efforts to Combat Corruption

Corruption is a global issue that poses significant challenges to the stability and integrity of financial systems worldwide. In recent years, there have been concerted efforts by international organizations, governments, and civil society to combat corruption and promote transparency and accountability. This subchapter explores the various global initiatives aimed at addressing corruption and their impact on the financial sector.

One of the key areas affected by corruption is global financial regulations. The revelations of high-profile financial scandals have exposed gaps in regulatory frameworks, prompting regulators to strengthen their oversight and adopt more stringent measures. International bodies such as the Financial Action Task Force (FATF) and the International Monetary Fund (IMF) have been actively involved in providing guidance and support to countries in enhancing their regulatory frameworks to combat money laundering and corruption.

The consequences of corruption are particularly evident in offshore tax havens. These jurisdictions, often characterized by weak regulations and secrecy, have become hotspots for illicit financial flows and tax evasion. As a result of global efforts, several countries have faced increased pressure to adhere to international standards and disclose information about offshore entities. This has led to a decline in the attractiveness of tax havens, as governments and regulators crack down on illicit activities.

The political fallout and resignations resulting from financial scandals have been significant. The exposure of corrupt practices has led to public outrage, loss of trust in institutions, and the resignation or dismissal of high-ranking officials. These events have highlighted the need for greater accountability and transparency in both the public and private sectors.

Legal actions and prosecutions against individuals involved in corruption have also gained traction. Governments and law enforcement agencies are increasingly cooperating across borders to investigate and prosecute corrupt individuals and entities involved in money laundering and bribery. These efforts serve as a deterrent and send a strong message that corruption will not be tolerated.

Reforms in corporate transparency and accountability have been another crucial aspect of global efforts. Companies are now required to disclose more information about their ownership, operations, and financial transactions. This increased transparency helps identify and prevent corrupt practices, ensuring a more level playing field for businesses and investors.

The role of whistleblowers and investigative journalism in exposing corruption cannot be overstated. Whistleblowers play a vital role in uncovering wrongdoing, and their protection and support are crucial for effective anti-corruption efforts. Investigative journalists also play a significant role in exposing corruption scandals, holding those involved accountable, and raising public awareness.

The impact of corruption on international relations and diplomacy should not be underestimated. Countries that fail to address corruption effectively may face reputational damage and strained relations with their international counterparts. International cooperation and dialogue are crucial in addressing cross-border corruption and fostering a culture of integrity.

The revelations of widespread corruption have also exposed the stark social and economic inequalities that exist in many societies. The concentration of wealth and privilege in the hands of a few has further eroded public trust and highlighted the need for more equitable distribution of resources.

Finally, the implications for money laundering and corruption are vast. Financial institutions have faced increased scrutiny and regulatory pressure to implement robust anti-money laundering measures. The exposure of corrupt practices has also led to the freezing and repatriation of illicit assets, further reinforcing the message that corruption will not go unpunished.

In conclusion, global efforts to combat corruption have gained momentum in recent years. The impact on global financial regulations, consequences for offshore tax havens, political fallout and resignations, legal actions and prosecutions, reforms in corporate transparency and accountability, social and economic inequality, role of whistleblowers and investigative journalism, effects on international relations and diplomacy, public perception of wealth and privilege, and implications for money laundering and corruption are all intertwined. It is crucial for bank regulators to stay abreast of these developments and actively contribute to the global fight against corruption. Only through collaborative efforts can we hope to create a more transparent, accountable, and just financial system.

Conclusion: Lessons Learned and the Path Forward for Bank Regulators

The financial scandals that have plagued the global banking industry in recent years have left a lasting impact on various aspects of society. As bank regulators, it is crucial for us to reflect on the lessons learned from these scandals and chart a path forward that ensures a more transparent and accountable financial system. In this conclusion, we will discuss the key takeaways from these scandals and outline the steps that need to be taken to address the challenges they have presented.

One of the most significant lessons learned is the need for enhanced global financial regulations. The scandals have exposed weaknesses in the current regulatory framework, allowing illicit activities to flourish. It is imperative that bank regulators collaborate across borders to develop stricter regulations that can prevent such misconduct in the future. This includes sharing information, harmonizing regulatory standards, and conducting regular audits to identify potential risks.

The consequences of these scandals for offshore tax havens cannot be ignored. These havens have been exploited by individuals and corporations to evade taxes and engage in illicit financial activities. Bank regulators must work towards closing loopholes and enforcing stricter regulations in these jurisdictions to prevent further abuse.

The political fallout and resignations resulting from these scandals have shaken public trust in the banking industry. Bank regulators must take decisive actions to restore confidence by holding those responsible accountable. Legal actions and prosecutions should be pursued vigorously to ensure that individuals involved in financial misconduct face appropriate consequences.

Reforms in corporate transparency and accountability are also crucial. Bank regulators should advocate for greater transparency in financial transactions, including the disclosure of beneficial ownership, to prevent money laundering and corruption. Strengthening corporate governance and implementing stricter internal controls within financial institutions will help mitigate the risk of future scandals.

The scandals have brought to light the deep-rooted issues of social and economic inequality. Bank regulators must address these disparities by promoting inclusive growth and ensuring fair access to financial services. This includes supporting initiatives that provide financial education and opportunities for marginalized communities.

The role of whistleblowers and investigative journalism in uncovering these scandals cannot be overstated. Bank regulators should encourage and protect whistleblowers, providing them with the necessary legal protections and incentives to come forward with information. Collaborating with investigative journalists can also help shed light on potential misconduct and hold wrongdoers accountable.

The effects of these scandals on international relations and diplomacy cannot be ignored. Bank regulators must work to rebuild trust and cooperation with other countries to prevent the exploitation of the financial system for illicit purposes. Strengthening international cooperation and information sharing will be crucial in this regard.

Public perception of wealth and privilege has been significantly affected by these scandals. Bank regulators must actively engage with the public and communicate their efforts to address the issues at hand. By demonstrating a commitment to transparency, accountability, and fairness, regulators can rebuild public trust and perception.

Lastly, the implications for money laundering and corruption must be addressed. Bank regulators should enhance their anti-money laundering frameworks, including the implementation of robust customer due diligence measures and the use of advanced technology to detect suspicious activities. Cooperation with law enforcement agencies and international bodies dedicated to combating corruption will also be essential.

In conclusion, the financial scandals have presented bank regulators with significant challenges. However, by learning from the lessons of the past and taking proactive steps, regulators can pave the way for a more accountable and transparent financial system. The path forward requires collaboration, stricter regulations, enhanced transparency, and a commitment to addressing social and economic inequality. By embracing these changes, bank regulators can restore trust, foster economic stability, and safeguard the integrity of the global financial system.

www.ingramcontent.com/pod-product-compliance
Lightning Source LLC
Chambersburg PA
CBHW021212160726
47994CB00001B/443